a tribute to
FRANKIE LAINE

Published by

CELEBRITY
PROFILES PUBLISHING
DIV. EDISON & KELLOGG
BOX 344 MAIN STREET
STONYBROOK, NEW YORK 11790-0344
(631) 862-8555 - F: (631) 862-0139
CELEBPRO4@AOL.COM
WWW.RICHARDGRUDENS.COM

Book Design and Editing by Madeline Grudens

Library of Congress Control Number in Progress

ISBN: 978-0-9763877-6-3
Printed in the United States of America
King Printing Company Inc.
Lowell, MA 01852

Books by Richard Grudens

The Best Damn Trumpet Player
The Song Stars
The Music Men
Jukebox Saturday Night
Snootie Little Cutie-The Connie Haines Story
Jerry Vale-A Singer's Life
The Spirit of Bob Hope
Magic Moments - The Sally Bennett Story
Bing Crosby - Crooner of the Century
Chattanooga Choo-Choo
(The Life and Times of the World
Famous Glenn Miller Orchestra)
The Italian Crooners Bedside Companion
When Jolson was King
Star*Dust - The Bible of the Big Bands
Mr. Rhythm - A Tribute to Frankie Laine

Frankie Laine

Mr. Rhythm

a tribute to

FRANKIE LAINE

TABLE OF CONTENTS

HENRY PLEASANTS

Henry Pleasants - Musical Historian: from **The Great American Popular Singers**.

"American lyricism as reflected in song, owes much to the Irish, the Scots and the Welsh, whose modes of speech are the most musical of the Anglican dialects; to the Jews, whose Yiddish is among the most musical of the German dialects, and to the Italians, whose contribution to American song from their native musicality is symbolized in the art of Frank Sinatra, Perry Como, Buddy Greco, Al Martino, and with new anglized names, Tony Bennett, Frankie Laine, Vic Damone and Dean Martin, among others."

PERRY COMO, FRANKIE LAINE AND FRANK SINATRA

MR. RHYTHM

FOREWORD

by Clint Eastwood

I first heard Frankie Laine when I was a kid. Of course, Frankie Laine came on with "That's My Desire," his big record. I remember I was living in Oakland, California - and everybody loved him - he became an overnight sensation with that record and then he had the ensuing "Shine" and "Kiss Me Again" and all these things did really well with everybody I knew. I know my early romantic life was definitely driven by Frankie Laine's records and if you could sit and hum "That's My Desire" to some gal, sometimes it had interesting results. Then he took another leap in his career when he came back with "Lucky Old Son" and" Mule Train." "Mule Train," I suppose, stimulated him to record great songs like "High Noon" later on, and then enabled him as the first choice to do records like "Rawhide."

After we were in production with *Rawhide* that had been written by Dimitri Tiomkin and Ned Washington, the same crew who had done "High Noon," had this title song "Rawhide" and Frankie Laine was going to sing it. So, I was very excited. I never thought that I would be in a picture that Frankie Laine would be singing in much less meeting him later on when Frankie and his lovely wife came on the show as guest actors. So it was a great thrill for me because he was a legend for me.

Frankie Laine was from a generation that doesn't exist anymore - the singers in those days all sang a lot - they were on the road, they had night club acts and appeared constantly all over. So everybody sang regularly and I think that's why there were so many great singers out of the '40s and '30s because they sang all the time. So singers were very 'trained up.'

In those days, people sang all the time. The women singers, the Peggy Lee's, the Dinah Shore's, the Doris Day's, all sang with bands so the bands toured and they were out every night singing. I remembered when I first met Frankie Laine I asked him, "When did you know "That's My Desire" would be a hit?" And he said: "Well, they suspected it," because every time he would do it as part of his night club act it would always get a tremendous reception. So he suspected that it would go and when it took off I guess they were not surprised.

I think Frankie's individuality - and they all had their own individual style and sound - that you knew who Frankie Laine was the moment he came on. You knew who Billy Eckstine was the moment he came on… Nat King Cole, Frank Sinatra…all of the singers of the '40s you knew them the moment you heard them - you could hear one bar and you would be off and running - you knew exactly who it was. You knew the difference between Ella and Sarah Vaughan - you knew the difference between Peggy Lee and Doris Day because it was a great era of music and unfortunately we're not in that great era of music right now, we're in an era which is mostly gimmickry and dictated by wardrobe. In those days all singers would come out and they would wear a suit and tie and musicians too - but there was nothing fancy - the signature was the sound and not so much the look.

So, when I was a kid listening in the car, with the old tube radios, listening to "That's My Desire" and with one hand on the wheel and the other around some young lady I was trying to be amorous with - I've got to thank Frankie Laine for those moments. I've got to thank him for all of the help he gave me in those days and later on when we got to work on *Rawhide* together. All of it was a great thrill for me and I'm very happy to be part of this tribute book about one of my great heroes, Frankie Laine.

INTRODUCTION

by Frank E. Dee - GMMY Radio

Frankie Laine: The Educator Of Good Song

Thanks be to God we have author Richard Grudens who continues to keep the singing legends and big bands of songs alive in our hearts and mind. One of those legendary singers of our time was Frankie Laine, who could sing it all; jazz, popular, country western, and blues. I may add the man never spared the vocal horses.

I have always said and believed that Crooners Croon and Singers Sing. In my opinion, Frankie Laine was indeed *the Singer*. As a matter of fact he was one of the greatest popular singers of our time. He had a marvelous well placed *Belcanto* singing voice. The word *Belcanto* translated from Italian to English means *Good Singing*. Frankie Laine knew just how to use the Belcanto style and project his powerhouse voice with ease. Those low and top notes were incredible. When he sang, he possessed the power to lure you into a melodic, nostalgic mode.

As a teenager of 14 years of age, during the summer of 1949, I never forgot the first time hearing Frankie Laine sing one of his big hit songs "That Lucky Old Sun" on a wind-up Victrola. Recordings, in those days, were on a 78RPM shellac record. Well, I just about wore this record out by playing it for hours over and over to the point which I practically drove my parents out of the house. It is safe to say that I was bitten by a bug of new and some good music, thanks to Frankie Laine. For me, he became the stepping stone to future good music and, even now, I have never stopped playing those wonderful recordings.

In the '70s I had my own radio show and often dedicated fifteen minutes of his songs played weekly at the former radio station WHET, in Waltham, Massachusetts.

Today, the voice of Frankie Laine is a mainstream feature daily on International GMMY Radio. His recordings are aired several times a day. Thank you Mr. Frankie Laine for being the iconoclast of good music.

FRANKIE LAINE
DECLARED A NATIONAL TREASURE

TRIBUTE TO FRANKIE LAINE
HON. RANDY `DUKE' CUNNINGHAM
United States Congressman - House of Representatives
(Extension of Remarks - March 25, 1993)

"Mr. Speaker, I rise today to pay tribute to a true American original, Frankie Laine, of San Diego, California, who celebrates his 80th birthday Tuesday, March 30, 1993.

"With a song in his heart and a bold, strong voice, Frankie Laine revives the old spirit of the American frontier. He reminds us of a time when the work was hard and the pleasures and conveniences of life were few, but simple; a time of `Rawhide' and `Mule Trains'; a time we sometimes forget, but for the timeless music of Frankie Laine, we warmly remember again.

"One would think that following a career gilded with 21 gold records, Frankie Laine would ease into retirement. Not so. In his adopted hometown of San Diego, Frankie has provided shoes to the homeless, friendship to the friendless, and countless hours of selfless service to the community and to the Salvation Army. The man called the Squire of Point Loma has been a prince of a good neighbor.

"On his 80th birthday, Tuesday, March 30, 1993, let it be recorded in the permanent Record of the Congress of the United States that Frankie Laine is a national treasure, an American original, and a great and generous friend to the people of this Nation."

Frank Paul Lo Vecchio Takes to the Mike

Backstage with Richard Grudens at Westbury Music Fair, 1984

It's difficult for me to believe that my friend of over 25 years, Frankie Laine, almost gave up on his struggling singing career, actually taking out two-and-a-half years to work at a defense plant where he earned a steady sixty-eight dollars a week. Then with a few bucks in his pocket, returned to the fray to try again but promising himself to quit if he did not succeed on his next, final bid.

But, of course, he probably would never have quit no matter what he may have thought at the time. I think I knew Frank pretty well over the many years of our friendship, and can say for certain his determination and dedication to his craft were always unwavering, good times and bad. The admirable way Frank has conducted his personal and professional life in every respect since his very first success in 1946 at that infamous Hollywood hangout on Vine Street, Billy Berg's, I'm sure, with dedication and his exemplary motivation, he would have persisted until his career turned itself around: hence "I was invited to sit in one night and I came away with good luck for a change by singing "Old Rocking Chair's Got Me." My luck turned, because a guy in the audience got very excited about the way I sang it. He turned out to be the song's composer, Hoagy Carmichael, (also the composer of the most standard of standards 'Star-

Hoagy Carmichael

dust') who convinced Billy to give me a job singing at seventy-five dollars a week."

Frank was the first he-man singer.... other than country-western singers--- who the blue-collar guys could identify with, but he really had a difficult time and some bad luck along the way. "Earlier, "he went on, "my friend, bandleader Jean Goldkette, got me a job at NBC, but England decided to declare war on Germany that day and my job went out the window. Hell, I was already 26 years old then. I hung around Ted Weems' band while my pal Perry Como was his singer. Perry recommended me for his replacement when he was leaving, but Weems didn't accept it, (Frank sang "Never In A Million Years" at his audition, which turned out to be prophetic) so Perry got me a job with his old boss, bandleader Freddie Carlone. That lasted just a few weeks because my jazz style didn't match his sweet Guy Lombardo type of band."

Frank's style was very innovative, which was why he had such difficulty with early acceptance. He would bend notes and sing about the chordal context of a note rather than to sing the note directly, and he stressed each rhythmic downbeat, which was different than the smoother balladeers of his time.

When Frankie sang at Cleveland's College in 1940, he intro-duced an unknown, starving singer, June Hart, who he really felt was terrific and badly needed a break. They ac... ... ... More bad luck while helping someone, but ... sang a ballad entitled "That's My Desire," w... but forgot about for six years.

"And how about the time I was ready ...ng a benefit at the Congress Hotel in Chicago when suddenly famed trumpet player Roy Eldridge showed up and decided to go into 'Body and Soul.' Who'd dare interrupt that for a punk kid nobody knew?"

For-tunately, Frankie decided to try out his new and terrific version of "That's My Desire," with head thrown back, eyes closed and mike in hand later at Billy Berg's. It brought down the house and began his climb up the proverbial ladder.

Then he began recording those he-man hits one after another, first with Mercury and then Columbia under the tutelage of Mitch Miller, namely "That's My Desire," then "Lucky Old Sun," "Jezebel," "Mule Train," "Shine," "High Noon," "Cry Of The Wild Goose," "Moonlight Gambler," and "Rawhide" .... all memorable ---all number-one smash hits, and to prove his bona fide affinity to country music, how about his definitive interpretation of Hank Williams' "Your Cheatin' Heart."

But, as good as they were, I prefer Frank's inspiring, early rendition of "We'll Be Together Again," (which he wrote with his lifelong friend, Carl Fischer) and the inspirational "I Believe," (written by our mutual friend Ervin Drake), Frank's own personal favorite and actually an expression of his life's definition.

with Helen O'Connell Backstage

I first saw Frankie Laine at the New York Paramount in 1947. He was on the in-person show (singing) with Ray McKinley, and comedian Billy De-Wolfe during the run of the movie "Golden Earrings." My first close up and personal meeting with Frank was in 1983 backstage at New York's Westbury Music Fair. He was appearing with his discovery, and now old compatriot, former Jimmy Dorsey song-star Helen O'Connell, Buddy Morrow, (who was fronting the Tommy Dorsey *ghost band*), and the legendary William B. Williams of New York's WNEW and it's famous radio show, *Make Believe Ballroom.* We hit it off like old friends at a reunion. After a few hours together we rounded up Helen O'Connell from the ladies dressing room and cleared up how he first discovered Helen:

"Well, Jimmy Dorsey's secretary, Nita Moore, and I were having breakfast and she told me that Jimmy was looking for a girl singer." Helen smiled in agreement.

"It happened that I saw Helen the night before singing at the Village Barn down on Eighth Street and I told Nita about her and Jimmy went to see her that night, and that's how he got Helen O'Connell." Helen was standing right next to me and Frank when he related that story with Helen nodding approval, then snuggling up and planting a kiss on Frank's blushing cheek.

Then Frank recounted his phenomenal success while appearing in England, where he was always so revered. On opening night at the Palladium, August 18, 1952, he broke the attendance record previously held by Judy Garland and Danny Kaye. He was sold out for the entire length of his two week stay, and even filled the standing room only areas, which were sold the day of each show, thereby selling out the fastest ever in the theater's history. The crowds milled outside the Palladium before each show to hopefully catch an up-close glimpse of this new powerhouse star from across the ocean-this new guy with the booming voice-Frankie Laine.

Nan and Frank were thrilled to death. It was so much more than they expected being so far from home. One afternoon Frank received a phone call from Columbia Records producer Mitch Miller, reporting his recording of "Mule Train" and "High Noon" that were released in the states were a smash. So, Carl Fischer improvised an arrangement from what he remembered of "Mule Train" and the next evening they introduced the song into the act. The audience went wild.

Frank moved on to Glasgow, Scotland, opening at the Empire Theater to an incredible reception. A crowd of over five-thousand gathered outside their hotel, and would not go away until Frank stepped out on the balcony to sing a few bars of "Rock Of Gibraltar," a song that went over big in Britain.

From there Frank and Nan went on to Italy to sing" Jezebel" to a

screaming crowd everywhere he traveled in his parents place of birth. Appearances in Milan, Venice, Florence, and Rome, where crowds topped each previous performance, were equally exciting for the traveling performer from America. He and Nan were genuinely overwhelmed at all the attention given them overseas.

In France, where he renewed his friendship with singer, Edith Piaf, known to the world as *The Little Sparrow,* Frankie and Nan were followed by crowds of fans everywhere they visited.

"Jezebel" had also reached France and became an instant hit.

Over the years, Frank returned to Europe to even greater successes. He has recorded hundreds of titles, and his international record sales exceeded the one-hundred million mark long ago.

Paramount Theater, New York - 1947

In his book *That Lucky Old Son*, Frank recalls that special feeling, corny though he thought it was, on returning a success to New York, where he once deeply felt the lowest point of his career, perhaps, even the low point of his life.

"I promised myself that I would never come back to New York unless I could do it on a *white horse*." Frank couldn't forget the nights sleeping in Central Park and those days that dragged by for him without food and for a long period.

"That's why I made it a point to treat myself to one very special evening during my first run at the Paramount Theater in New York. I spent it alone. I dressed in a custom made suit and a camel hair overcoat and headed for Central Park. There, I sought out the dilapidated bench that had once been my bed. I sat down and dined on a candy bar and thought about the time when penny candy bars were all I could afford to eat. In one of my pockets was a wallet packed with more money than I ever had before. In the other a key to one of the most comfortable hotel suites in New York. After that short contemplation I hailed a taxi and was chauffered to the heart of Times Square where my name appeared in big, beautiful lights and where they were paying me $2,500 a week to do what I loved best." Frank hopes that everybody, at least once in their lives, know such a moment for themselves.

In 1985, while I was writing a monthly column called "Jazz and Jazzmen" for *Long Island P.M. Magazine,* Frank fell ill needing a quadru-

Frankie Laine

March 6, 1985

Dear Richard:

Thank you so much for your letter of
February 16th and thank you for
encouraging fans to write. I did
receive many cards and that was
a great help to me at a very low
time in my life.

I'm happy to report that I'm feeling
better every day and do hope to be
able to start singing again later
this year.

Thanks again and my very best to you.

Gratefully,

Frank

Frankie Laine

ple-bypass heart operation. I let the readers know and encouraged them
to write cheerful letters to Frank at his home that overlooked beautiful San
Diego, California harbor. He was so grateful.

Frank had a remarkable recovery and by the time 1990 rolled

around, he had completed his fifth year since that surgery, but in April of 1990, he had to have a triple bypass. In 1991, however, Frank was having some throat troubles and took a year off. His good wife of then 42 years, the movie actress Nan Grey, had troubles with her vision which, by way of two operations, was fully restored to 20/20.

A few years later, with Nan gone: "Nan's special way of touching my life will remain in my heart forever and permits me to move on to continue my work. I believe," he said so sincerely, "God is everywhere. You don't have to go to church to find him."

Frank had one of the biggest hearts in show business and one of the smallest egos. We lost a great human being in 2007 when we lost Frankie Laine. He was ninety-four. He had just finished the notes for the introduction of my book, *Stardust*.

Frank's last words in his own book are: "Like the song says ...the music never ends."

That's the best legacy Frankie Laine can ever give.

MATERNAL GRANDFATHER
SALVATORE SALERNO

THE WEDDING OF
FRANKIE'S
PARENTS, 1910
MR. & MRS. GIOVANNI
LO VECCHIO

FAMILY FACTS

Francesco Lo Vecchio - Family Facts

- Francesco's parents emigrated from the Sicilian village of Monreale, Italy near Palermo.

- His family settled in Chicago's "Little Italy."

- Francesco Paolo Lo Vecchio, the oldest of eight children, born in Chicago on March 30, 1913 on the 2nd story of a small house on Townsend Street.

- His siblings were Rose, Sam, Joe, John, Rose, Gloria, and Phil.

- Rose died of Diphtheria in 1917, at the age of two.

- Frankie's father was, for a time, personal barber to the gangster Al Capone.

- Grandfather Salerno was shot and killed by the mob, although he was the peacemaker among the rival mobs. Frankie witnessed the killing.

- Frankie attends Immaculate Conception Elementary School and joins the choir.

- He is electrified by Al Jolson's appearance in *The Singing Fool* singing "Sonny Boy" While attending Lane Technical High School, he is influenced by Louis Armstrong's "West End Blues" and recordings of blues singer Bessie Smith.

FRANKIE - AGE 6

- Frankie begins singing anywhere and everywhere and anytime anyone would listen.

- Attending the Merry Garden Ballroom where the Joe Kayser Orchestra performed with Gene Krupa on Drums, Frankie Trumbauer on Sax, Frank Teschemacher on clarinet, Muggsy Spanier on trumpet, became another great musical influence.

- Attended personal appearance of Paul Whiteman's King of Jazz Orchestra. He watched and was mesmerized by first female big band singer Mildred Bailey singing Hoagy Carmichael's "Rockin' Chair."

- Before his association with the grueling Marathon Days, Frankie Lo Vecchio took a job at International Harvester Company for fifteen dollars a week working in the Mailroom.

- Soon, unemployed again, and out of money, and at a loss, when a marathon dance company comes to Chicago.

Here is the rest of the story:

Frank with his Parents

The Lo Vecchio Family (Nan Grey - lower left)

DANCE MARATHON DAYS

Is Bing Listening?

The Marathon dancing craze became popular in the 1920s and 1930s. People who were without standard employment were invited to compete in the contests to hopefully win money or perhaps achieve fame. But it wasn't easy.

As Jazz singer Anita O'Day described in her biography *High Times, Hard Times*: "It seems unbelievable now but there were once fifteen thousand people-- promoters, emcees, floor judges, trainers, nurses, cooks, janitors, cashiers, ticket-takers, publicity agents, promotion men, musicians, contestants and even a lawyer-- whose main source of income over a number of years came from endurance (Marathon dancing) shows."

Anita O'Day

During my interview with Anita in the mid-nineties, she described her involvement with the marathon competitions, something she had in common with Frankie Laine and other entertainers who were just getting into show business and used the marathons as a catalyst.

"All I had to do was have a doctor take my blood pressure, listen to my heartbeat -then they sent in a nurse of sorts to check me out for lice, crabs and other body vermin. When I objected, she said, 'Listen, sweetheart, it's for your own protection." The regulars welcomed it. Everybody's in close contact in a jackpot like this."

Frankie Laine entered the marathon dancing craze to earn money and as a hopeful stepping stone to advance his show business dreams. There were several ways you could earn money. One, was to enter dancing contests and keep dancing until you

On horseback with partner Ruth Smith after they set the world's record for Marathon Dancing at Young's Million Dollar Pier in Atlantic City, 1932

broke away- or ran out of steam. Second, entertain the people who came to watch the events. Frankie did a little of both, beginning first with singing before almost ten thousand people on his first event.

"One night there was a *Night of Stars*, a charity event that attracted every kind of act. There were talented actors and there were amateurs, who were just couples with the hope of enduring long enough to win money or a prize. That night I was called upon to sing in front of 10,000 skeptics. I was just seventeen. Jess Stacy, a piano player who later joined the Benny Goodman band, said to me, 'What would you like to sing, kid?

"I choose 'Beside An Open Fireplace,' a popular song at the time, written by bandleader Will Osborne. Jess asked me to select a 'key, ' which puzzled me. We tried E flat, an easy key for me to sing in.'" 'Fireplace' was a very sentimental tune. When I finished the crowd became quiet. Then some broke out into tears, as did I. Then a reaction I did not expect. The crowd turned to yelling and cheering and foot stomping."
I felt ten feet high and they wanted more. Jess struck up the band with 'Coquette' and five more encores. This was at the Merry Garden. So they hired me, but not as a singer, but as a *shepherd* and marathon trainer and also ran errands. I also had to keep a watch on the dancers who were

sleeping on cots during their break. It was there I learned the facts of life during the wee hours. I also was able to sing almost every night, learning songs like 'Body and Soul' and 'Stardust.'

"The time line here was November 1930, when Frankie decided to go to Baltimore with the contest manager, Eddie Gilmartin, as he promised Frankie to handle M.C. duties and use him as a trainer. Nobody had much of a job then so it was an opportunity for Frankie to work.

"I figured I could send money back home because we were in the depths of the depression and my family needed my (financial help). Pa didn't consider singing a practical ambition like a pharmacist or an architect, but Ma, God love her, supported me, so I was soon on my way to Baltimore."

Frank went to Baltimore where, at one point, he was a finalist and with a girl named Betty Jacobs, won after 106 grueling days.

" I was shocked that I could last." Frankie was handed $2,800.00 as his share of the prize money. When he returned home with all that cash in his hand, he was hailed as a hero to his family.

In 1932, with partner Ruth Laine set the world's record for Dancing at Young's Milllion in Atlantic City, New took a grand total hours, translat- 145 days. will find it in Guiness Book of World Re-

Smith, Frankie Marathon Dollar Pier Jersey. It of 3,500 ing to You the

cords.

Frank continued marathon dancing and entertaining. " I was singing mainly Bing Crosby tunes like 'I Surrender Dear' and 'Straight from the Shoulder.' Crooning was the current singing craze and I imitated Bing so closely that some said I sounded just like him."

Frankie Laine worked 14 marathons. Won some, lost some, but it was a crazy, but practical, although difficult way to earn a living during the Great Depression. Besides marathons and singing, Frankie was able to earn money selling picture postcards of himself.

With Bing Crosby

The Marathons became more brutal as time passed. Many participants hurt their ankles, and many became sick from exhaustion that led to further medical problems.

"Before I was finished with the craze I met a 14 year old in the contest who was a very good singer. She would follow me around like a puppy trying to learn how I sang, and breathed, and how I held notes so long, always asking me questions about singing. When management found she was underaged they yanked her off the floor fast. This budding singer eventually did pretty good for herself. Her name was Anita O'Day, one of America's great jazz singers."

Frankie Laine learned a lot and developed his skills during Marathon Days. It kept him inspired and hopeful and paved the way for his eventual success. He certainly had mastered endurance, important to a singer who at times had to perform for long hours in night clubs and theaters.

Frankie Laine and 52nd Street - The Street of Jazz

When Frankie was watching the greats playing the Sunday "jams" on Swing Street, that is, 52nd Street in New York City between 5th and 6th Avenues, he would hang around in one of the back booths waiting for a chance to sing. The customers would be three deep around the bar, nursing one drink for the entire afternoon.

Frankie Laine had a long run at the steakery, but it was under a special, strange arrangement.

"Somebody heard me sing in the Village at Bobby Hackett's place - Nick's, wasn't it? It was trumpeter Red Allen who said to me: 'Why don't you come up to the Hickory House on Sunday? They have these jams. When I get on the stand, I'll have Joe Marsala get you up.' Joe was an accomplished clarinetist and songwriter. ("Don't Cry Joe.")

"I figured, my God, maybe this is an omen. Joe Marsala was from Chicago. He lived in the same neighborhood as I did, just around the corner from where I went to school. We used to run around with the same crowd, except that he was older than our gang."

Frank couldn't wait for Sunday to come. When he got to the Hickory House, Red was already up on the stand playing. One of the things Frankie used to do was a great jazz version of 'Stardust.' Red tried to get Joe to get Frankie up on the stand. But Joe kept stalling and calling on other people. Frankie did not get upset because he was content watching Adele, a (Jazz) harp player he admired.

Finally, after a lull, Bobby Hackett, put down his trumpet, went up and played guitar. Frankie went up and sang two choruses of 'Stardust.' They were wild versions. Joe Marsala was excited and told Frankie to wait around.

"Listen, Frankie, " said Joe Marsala," I have no budget to pay anybody, but if you want to come around, I'll get you up every night. Somebody might hear you we'll go from there."

Frank spent eight months dressed in a tux every night and almost never got the chance to sing. He ran out of money and wrote his father who sent him a few hundred dollars so he could stay in New York. Frank was visibly upset when Marsala realized it and finally began to call him up, but to no avail.

"I hung around Hickory House from April 1937, until December." He went home for Christmas.

After that, it was a long time, and a long road before he released "That's My Desire," that made everyone notice. That was 10 years later. Frank figured he was too early with his style. Crooners Bing and Perry were in their prime. The belting approach that Frankie offered was too revolutionary. The story goes that Gene Krupa, the drummer, walked into the Hickory House the first night and was graced with a hundred-dollar bill and a new recording contract. Timing is everything.

Frankie Laine's time had not yet come at this point.

REMEMBERING FRANKIE

Venue Cymru, Llandudno
Friday 4th July 2008

"It is hard to imagine life without the National Youth Jazz Orchestra."
Ronald Atkins, The Guardian

"With players of this calibre the future of British jazz is in safe hands"
Tony Augarde, Oxford Times

"If there is a better band in Europe, I have yet to hear it"
John Martin, Jazz Rag

"NYJO is a National Musical Treasure"   *Ken Rattenbury, Crescendo*

"The perfect model of a big band"   *Peter Hepple, The Stage*

THE MUSICIANS

SPECIAL GUEST
JEFF HOOPER

SAXOPHONES
Ed Barker
Lucas Dodd
Richard Shepherd
Will Gibson
Tom Leaper

TROMBONES
Eoghan Kelly
Mat Walton
Joe Harries
Ross Anderson

TRUMPETS
Rob Greenwood
Tommy Walsh
Mark Perry
Henry Armburg-Jennings

RHYTHM SECTION
Jon Russell (Guitar)
Laurence Ungless (Bass)
Chris Eldred (Piano)
Scott Chapman (Drums)

VOCALS/ FLUTE
Sarah Ellen Hughes

MUSICAL DIRECTOR
BILL ASHTON MBE

SOUND
Theuns Van Dyk
Eben Wessels

NYJO's recordings will be on sale during the interval. The most recent CDs are: **The Very Best of NYJO"** (boxed set of 4 Cds), **"Something Old Something New"** featuring Atila, Paul Hart's **"Two Suites" and "London Pride"**. The DVD **"Out of Hamelin"** will also be available.

NYJO BY POST on page 38 of our magazine "News From NYJO" lists all our recordings, and explains how to become a **Friend of NYJO**. Details of how to join NYJO are on page 2.

THE MUSIC

A Foggy Day	arr. Steve Titchener
Embraceable You	arr. Ken Wheeler
One for Oscar	Andy Vinter
Almost There	Anthony Adams
What Am I Here For?	Frankie Laine: Duke Ellington
Let's Settle Down	Bill Ashton: arr. Evan Jolly
You'd Be So Nice To Come Home To	Cole Porter (Instrumental)
Where is The Music?	Long: Kitchen arr. Chris Smith

INTERVAL

A Woman in Love	Frank Loesser
That's My Desire	Carol Loveday: Helmy Kreser
Sunny Side of the Street	Jimmy McHugh: Dorothy Fields
All of Me	Seymour Simons: Gerald Marks
Georgia	Hoagy Carmichael
It Only Happens Once	Frankie Laine
We'll Be Together Again	Fisher/Laine arr. Nelson Riddle
Rawhide	Ned Washington: Dimitri Tiomkin
Taking a Chance on Love	Latouche:Fetter:Vernon Duke
S'Posin'	Paul Denniker: Andy Razaf
That Old Feeling	Lou Brown: Sammy Fain
Stars Fell On Alabama	Mitchell Parish: Frank Perkins
Jezebel	Wayne Shanklin

core:

I Believe   Erwin Drake, Irwin Graham, Jimmy Shirl, Al Stillman

ernatives

Pennies From Heaven	John Burke: Arthur Johnstone
If You Were Mine	Johnny Mercer : Matt Malneck
Roses of Picardy	Frederick Weatherly: Haydn Wood

Since 1965, Bill Ashton, the Orchestra's Musical Director, has argued the case that jazz deserves a place in the educational curriculum. Through the efforts of many like-minded and dedicated people, jazz has established itself as a serious subject in schools and colleges; indeed jazz is now an option within Music GCSE, and NYJO's own recordings have been used as the source material. NYJO's influence has also led to the formation of Jazz Orchestras all over the country.

An important part of NYJO's work is to provide workshops and rehearsals for young less experienced musicians.The concert personnel is selected from the pool of over 200 musicians currently committed to NYJO and NYJO 2. During the course of a year over 100 players will have performed concerts with NYJO.

Like so many Arts organisations, NYJO continues to exist through the goodwill, dedication and generosity of all those concerned with its well-being. Over the past 20 years NYJO has received major sponsorship from WH Smith, C&A, NatWest Bank, British Gas, Unison (matched by The Pairing Scheme for new Arts Sponsors) and The Worshipful Company of Musicians. We were also proud to have won a BP ABSA Award for the Best Use of Sponsorship Money.

NYJO continues to receive financial support from Arts Council England.
NYJO also receives assistance from the Musicians Benevolent Fund.
NYJO welcomes new sponsors. Please contact Bill Ashton MBE, Musical Director.

NYJO wishes to thank the following :
Yamaha and Fender Arbiter   -   for our PA system
AKG   -   for our microphones
Roland - for our Digital Piano
Trevor R James - for our Alto Flute
Barnes and Mullins - for percussion instruments
Ted Rockley of Klactoveesedstene - Honorary Design Consultant
Patrons - Anne Bertram Howard le Breton, Annette Armour,
Corporate Donors -   Bass plc, BP, Vauxhall.
Musicians' Benevolent Fund
The Musicians Union
Arts Council of England
Anglo-American Music Trust
The Board of Directors of NYJO
and our many <u>FRIENDS OF NYJO</u>

NYJO   11 VICTOR ROAD   HARROW   MIDDLESEX   HA2 6PT
www.NYJO.org.uk   bill.ashton@virgin.net   020 8863 2717

FRANKIE'S HEROES

Frankie with Al Jolson on the set of "Jolson Sings Again" - 1949

Two giants of jazz initially influenced Frankie Laine musically. One was Bessie Smith and the other was Al Jolson, known as the World's Greatest Entertainer.

God it is said, made Bessie Smith, Empress of the Blues, when He made Heaven and Earth, and in a wild, extraordinary moment he added the powerful vocal influences of Ma "Gertrude" Rainey, Mildred Bailey, Ethel Waters, Billie Holiday, Ella Fitzgerald, and Dinah Washington. A magnificent cornucopia of great jazz voices.

Frankie Laine felt the power of Bessie Smith more than anyone of this group when he heard her sing "Bleeding Heart Blues" with "Midnight Blues" on the other side.

" The first time I laid the needle down on that record I felt cold chills and an indescribable excitement." It was Frankie's first exposure to jazz and the blues.

Al Jolson, *The Jazz Singer*, was the other musical hero discovered when Frankie Laine skipped a class and went to see Jolson in the film *The Singing Fool*. "He electrified me with his delivery and power," said Frankie. Frankie was very impressed when Jolson went down on one knee and delivered the song "Sonny Boy." His heart swelled.

"Bessie Smith and Al Jolson really fueled my interest in music. I admired Jolson as a performer who could command an audience and Bessie as a great jazz artist. She thrilled me. She had music in her soul.

You have to place Louis Armstrong into the mix at this point. Frankie's excitement when listening to Louis' "West End Blues" sent him through the roof, as Frankie described it. Later, Frankie's first album included that very poignant Armstrong tune.

Now Frankie knew what he wanted to do for the rest of his life.

Bessie Smith

Bessie Smith

Mildred Bailey

MR. RHYTHM

Ethel Waters

Ella Fitzgerald

Dinah Washington

Billie Holiday

MERCURY AND COLUMBIA

with Mitch Miller

"In those days there were no music videos, so listeners would picture the singer in their mind's eye, and to a lot of people this new singer Frankie Laine was a black man singing his heart out."

"Frankie Laine always loved to sing. Nothing made him happier. To me, he was the 'working man's singer' with a great ability to communicate the emotions of the common man," said Mitch Miller during Frankie Laine's recording days.

"After my stint at the Paramount I went back to Mercury Records and found I had a new A & R man assigned to me by the name of

Mitch Miller. I had been living off the last session when we recorded 'Shine,' which remained on the charts for thirty-five weeks."

At the time, Mitch Miller was actually a classical musician and one of the best oboist's in America. He was associated with the Rochester Symphony and the Eastman School of Music, a music conservatory located in Rochester, New York that was established in 1921. It was founded by George Eastman of Kodak Camera fame. It has been compared to New York's Juilliard School and, in Boston, the Berklee School of Music.

Frank won-dered what a classically trained musi-cian could possible do for him.

Well, the two got along very well. Mitch also understood that Frankie needed Carl Fischer as his partner, and Miller respected this. Mitch Miller had a knack for setting up uncanny musical voices in a very original way. When Frankie and Mitch settled down and worked on a few new songs, Mitch found a tune that he felt was a combination of the songs "Old Man River" and " Black and Blue."

"It wasn't really jazz," said Frankie, "but it had a Western flavor.

with Columbia Studio Execs

And so this was our first association and it was a great one."

The song was "That Lucky Old Sun." Frank then toyed with over a dozen new songs that went nowhere. He figured that if Mitch Miller could come up with his first one and it was a big hit, that he should let Mitch chose the songs. It turned out to be a good idea. Subsequently, Mitch brought him four million sellers in a row.

"Mitch wanted me to record a cowboy song and I refused, figuring I'd lose my 'Desire' and 'Lucky Old Sun' fans.

"Frank, I've listened to you sing and I know what you are capable of, so let me play it for you again. Give it a try."

" I felt I owed him one so I went along. Carl agreed with me. I had to record on a Sunday because I was opening in Minneapolis on Saturday and Detroit on Monday, so we flew in to record this new song."

At the studio, Mitch said, "Frank, this is another 'Lucky Old Sun,'

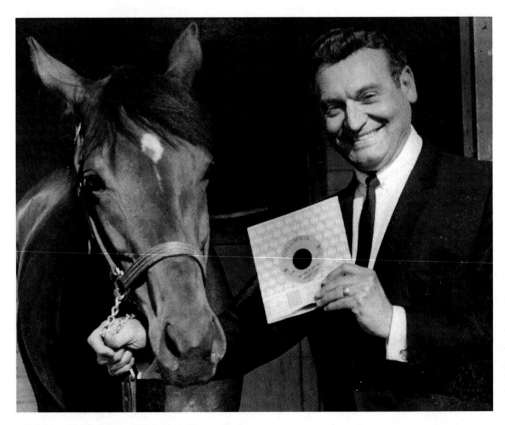

Frankie with his Mule and Mule Train Recording!

MR. RHYTHM

Mitch Miller and Frankie at Columbia

mark my words. I know you think this is not your kind of material, but I think it's great for you."

The song was "Mule Train."

Mitch Miller followed up with "Swamp Girl," and "Cry of the Wild Goose," all being four million sellers in a row."

Mitch Miller switched over to Columbia about the same time Frankie's contract with Mercury was up in March, 1951. Miller succeeded Mannie Sachs. The first song Mitch came up with for Frankie was another blockbuster "Jezebel."

By now, these three were a working team: "Mitch, Carl, and I got together to plan my show when I opened at the Copacabana in New York."

After Frankie got back from his European tour, Mitch Miller was ready for him with a basket full of new ideas. "He tried out some of them, including recording duets with other Columbia artists. I once did a duet with Patti Page at Mercury, but at Columbia I was able to duet with Doris

Day, Jo Stafford, The Four Lads and even Johnnie Ray, Mitch had also brought me 'Someday,' and the re-worked classic 'Granada.'"

Mitch Miller felt so strong about Frankie's ability to put over Ervin Drake's tune "I Believe" that he flew out to California just to present it to him in person.

"Mitch sang the first four bars, and Mitch cannot sing, but I could

Frankie Laine

October 20, 1998

Dear Rich,

Mitch Miller and I were together for ten years. In those ten years he turned out to be the greatest A & R man with whom I was ever lucky enough to be associated, and I had worked with a lot of them.

He had an unerring instinct for picking the right song for the right person at the right time. He brought me "High Noon," "I Believe," "Cheatin' Heart," "Lucky Old Sun," "Moonlight Gambler," "Hey, Joe," "Hawkeye," "Someday," "Mule Train," "Swamp Girl," "Cry Of The Wild Goose" and many others too numerous to mention. Most of these turned out to be million sellers in their time.

I will be forever grateful to Mitch.

Best regards,

Frankie Laine

Frankie Laine

Rosemary Clooney, Frank and DJ Peter Potter

sense its worth in spite of his performance. The song was like a prayer. The song didn't just speak to me, it spoke for me."

The song "Rawhide" was the last professional association Frankie Laine had with Mitch Miller. Mitch, like Carl Fischer, brought to Frankie's life a rewarding musical experience that enhanced his life.

Mitch Miller also contributed immensely to the lives of a group of other singers just about everyone knows. Who else would've put a harpsichord on a Rosemary Clooney record, or backed Guy Mitchell with swooping French Horns.

When Mitch moved to Columbia, besides selecting super hits for Frankie Laine, he selected "Singing the Blues" for Guy Mitchell, "Cold, Cold, Heart" for Tony Bennett, "Cry" and "Just Cryin' in the Rain" for Johnnie Ray, "Two Purple Shadows" for Jerry Vale and "American Beauty Rose" for Frank Sinatra.

Mitch Miller's own hit recordings with his Mitch Miller and the Gang show began in 1950 with his adaptation of the Israeli folk song "Tzena, Tenza, Tzena" with a choral background, which became his signature.

Songs like "The Yellow Rose of Texas" and "The Children's Marching Song" from the film The Inn of the Sixth Happiness, were great Miller successes.

Over later years Mitch Miller spent his time mainly directing George Gershwin works in various symphony halls, an endeavor bringing him back to his early classical roots. This wonderful man, contributor to much of our popular music through the voices like Frankie Laine, lives in New York City and is in his nineties.

You cannot overstate Mitch Miller's contribution to popular music.

Mitch Miller and Frankie

Carl Fischer and Frankie

CARL FISCHER

Frankie Laine had a faithful friend in a thin, trim, talented, personable and talented Native American - Cherokee Indian - by the name of Carl Fischer. Carl was searching for a song-writing partner. He had written the song "Who Wouldn't Love You" with lyricist Bill Carey who just went into the Army. The Maritime Service on Catalina Island, located off the coast of California, employed Carl. When he first met Frankie Laine Carl was playing piano for Ted Weems. He was currently on a ten-day furlough. Their first meeting was held at a Nat "King" Cole rehearsal, and yielded nothing in particular except that Carl produced a demonstration record without words, of course,

and played it for Frank. Although Frank was able to read music, he was not able to write it. He very much liked the composition. Carl told him not to be concerned and that the actual writing of a manuscript would be his responsibility. Carl was looking for ideas and someone who could write lyrics to his music.

It became their first collaboration, and was entitled "We'll Be Together Again." However, it did take Frankie six months from his first word to the last word to complete the song, but, Oh! what a wonderful song!

"Carl and I formed a partnership that lasted ten years. He was my friend, partner, and musical inspiration, until the day he died.

"And he died so young!"

Frankie Laine began singing regularly at Billy Berg's on March 6,1946 and Carl Fischer was medically discharged from the service a few days later. They were now able to get together to work on some new tunes. It was during the time Frank was still struggling and Berg's had just hired him.

Carl, Nan and Frankie

Carl and Frankie got together as serious partners right after Frankie received his first royalty check of $36,000 for "That's My Desire."

"The day before recording 'Desire' I was in debt for seven thousand dollars. I needed to get a perspective on all of this, so I asked Carl Fischer for a meeting in my dressing room and explained to him that if I was capable of earning this kind of money, the question became, 'How long would this last?'"

"Frank," Carl said softly, "from what I hear every night and from what I see in the eyes of your fans, I think you have a good chance to go all the way for as long and as far as you want to go."

While recording albums at Mercury, Carl constantly had to scratch out little parts for the various pickup musicians who frequently came and left. He was now Frankie's musical director and arranger.

Carl rehearsing Frankie

Carl was there with Frankie when, in 1947, Frankie headlined at the Paramount, thanks to Woody Herman who had set it up for him.

After the Paramount and working up some of the songs that made Frankie Laine a great star, it seemed as if nothing could go wrong. They were on a roller coaster with great songs under their belt and a brilliant future.

March 27, 1954 was, as Frankie called it, the blackest day of his life. It was sudden and devastating.

"My dear friend Carl Fischer had a heart attack and passed before my eyes. He was feeling pain early in the evening and his arm went numb. He lay down to sleep, rolled over on his stomach and dropped off to sleep and never awakened."

Carl was gone. Nan received the news first and reached Frankie at the golf course next morning. Carl was only 41 years old. Frankie raced over to the Fischer home in Sherman Oaks. Frankie canceled all his upcoming concerts and for two weeks hardly speaking a word to anyone. To Frankie, Carl could never be replaced. He was a brother, a mentor, and a right arm, whose love for the music was as strong as his own. The two had gone through so much together. How could this be?

Al Lerner: "Frankie Laine hired me to be his piano accompanist and I could see his pain and hear it in his songs. He tried hard to be strong. When the curtain of the first show we did together was lowered Frankie broke down and cried after singing an emotional version of "Jealousy" that Carl had arranged.

Life had changed for Frankie Laine. Nan convinced him that he had to go on so that all the work they did together wasn't wasted.

Frankie had resurrected a composition Carl had composed. A friend, Victor Young, who composed music for the films The Quiet Man and Samson & Delilah, sat down and scored the composition called "War Dance" and arranged to premier it with the Cleveland Symphony Orchestra on August 5, 1954.

It was a fine tribute to Carl Fischer. Frankie and Nan felt the wonder of it while sitting in the audience with Carl's wife, Terry, and their two daughters, Carol and Terry, listening to a seventy-piece orchestra perform the composition in front of ten thousand people. The recording of the piece was eventually released by Columbia Records

Ray Barr

Frank acquired a wonderful new musical director in Ray Barr. They were already good friends and he reminded him a lot of Carl. "So Ray took over as my full-time arranger, conductor and accompaniest."

It remained that way very happily for over 20 years.

STRIKING GOLD

FRANKIE LAINE'S GOLD RECORDS

Definition of a gold record before December, 1974 meant that one million copies were sold as singles, albums were at 500,000.

1. THAT'S MY DESIRE - 1946, MERCURY 5007

2. ON THE SUNNY SIDE OF THE STREET - 1947, MERCURY 1027.

3. TWO LOVES HAVE I - 1947, MERCURY 5064

4. SHINE - 1947, MERCURY 5091c

5. THAT LUCKY OLD SUN - 1949, MERCURY 5316

6. MULE TRAIN - 1949, MERCURY 5345

7. CRY OF THE WILD GOOSE - 1950, MERCURY 5363

8. SWAMP GIRL - 1950, MERCURY 5390

9. JEZEBEL - 1951, COLUMBIA 139367

10. ROSE, ROSE, I LOVE YOU - 1951, COLUMBIA 139367 (B)

11. JEALOUSY - 1951, COLUMBIA

12. HIGH NOON - 1952, COLUMBIA 39770

13. SUGARBUSH - 1952, COLUMBIA

14. I BELIEVE - 1953, COLUMBIA 39938

15. YOUR CHEATIN' HEART - 1953, COLUMBIA 39938

16. KID'S LAST FIGHT - 1954, COLUMBIA 40178

17. COOL WATER - 1955, COLUMBIA 40457

18. A WOMAN IN LOVE - 1955, COLUMBIA 40583

19. MOONLIGHT GAMBLER - 1956, COLUMBIA 40780

20. RAWHIDE - 1958, COLUMBIA 41230

21. LORD YOU GAVE ME A MOUNTAIN - 1969, ABC RECORDS 11174

22. MAKING MEMORIES - 1967, ABC RECORDS 10924

FRANKIE'S

GOLD

with Paul Weston & Jo Stafford

MR. RHYTHM

NAN GREY

How To Live Together for Forty Years

Nan Grey was an accomplished actress who fell in love with Frankie Laine, married him in 1950, and remained married to him the rest of her life, until her passing in 1994. Nan quit her lucrative film career and was content to spend her life with her hero, Frankie Laine.

Nan's maiden name was Eschol Loleet Miller and, earlier was married to a horse jockey Jackie Westrope back in 1939.

Nan graced twenty-five films from 1934 through 1941 and played the lead in the soap opera *Those We Love*. Her major films were *Three Smart Girls* and *Three Smart Girls Grow Up*, and *Tower of London* with Vincent Price and Basil Rathbone.

"The backstage note said she wanted to meet me because it was her birthday and attendance at my show was a present," Frankie explained. "Apparently she'd flipped the first time she heard 'That's My Desire' on the radio. When I came out to meet her, it was my turn to flip."

Frankie certainly knew who she was, remembering her role in the movie *Three Smart Girls* alongside Oscar winning singer Deanna Durbin. "Boy, was she pretty. Our personalities clicked and we hit it off nicely." After an unavoidable, but short, show business separation, a second meeting spawned a romance that led to marriage.

"Nan's beautiful daughters Pamela and Jan were like my own. We became a special family."

The honeymoon had them flying to Argentina, in South America. "Unfortunately, Nan came down with an emergency appendicitis that forced us back to Beverly Hills ahead of schedule."

Frank's extensive, well-planned tour led them overseas to England and Scotland, starting in 1952. Nan always loved traveling and was happy to be with Frank and witness his great success. It began with two record-breaking weeks at the London Palladium, continued on to Paris, France, and Italy, in Milan, Venice, Florence, and Rome.

Nan loved to peruse the antique shops wherever they went and sent home bundle after bundle of marvelous designer artifacts and decorative presents for their home.

Nan Grey had appeared in thirty-six films.

In the 1960s Nan marketed a special cosmetic mirror for nearsighted women. Princess Grace was one of her customer's.

L-R: Pam, Jan, Nan and Frankie

The only time the Laine's worked together was in a television episode of *Rawhide* in 1960. She, as Carlie Evans in the story Incident on the *Road to Yesterday* with Frankie playing the role of her long lost lover.

In true life, however, they were always together and led happy lives.

"Nan's special way of touching each of our lives personally will remain in our hearts forever. We'll be together again," Frank said so sadly.

Four important points had governed their lives together:

1. Live and let live.
2. To each his own.
3. Do unto others as you would have others do unto you.
4. All things in moderation.

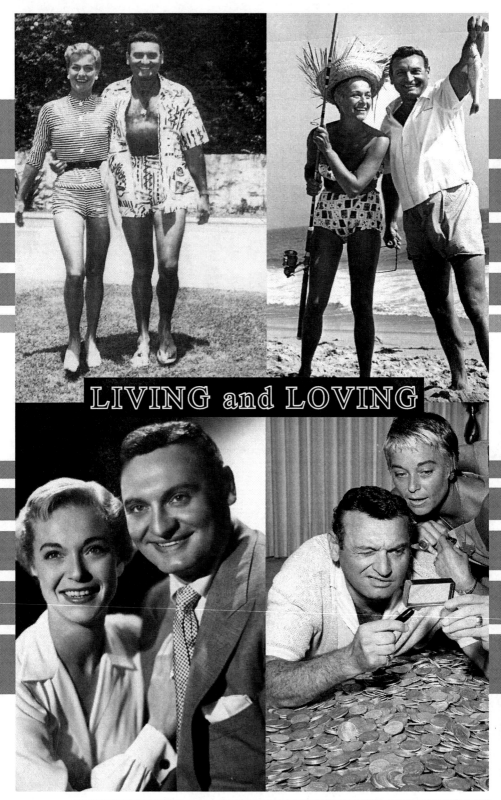

LIVING and LOVING

FRANKIE LAINE DIARY

The 1952 Frankie Laine Diary
Life on the stages of England and Europe

DOWNBEAT MAGAZINE VOL. 19 - NO. 25
CHICAGO, DECEMBER 17, 1952

FRANK'S EUROPEAN DIARY
THE EXCLUSIVE STORY OF THE LAINE'S TOUR
THROUGH BRITAIN, FRANCE & ITALY

On his overseas trip in 1952, Frankie Laine kept a diary.
Here it is in its entirety in Frankie Laine's own written words.
The text is exactly written as shown with nothing added,
nothing changed or omitted. Days that were skipped had no
entries documented.

Leaving for England

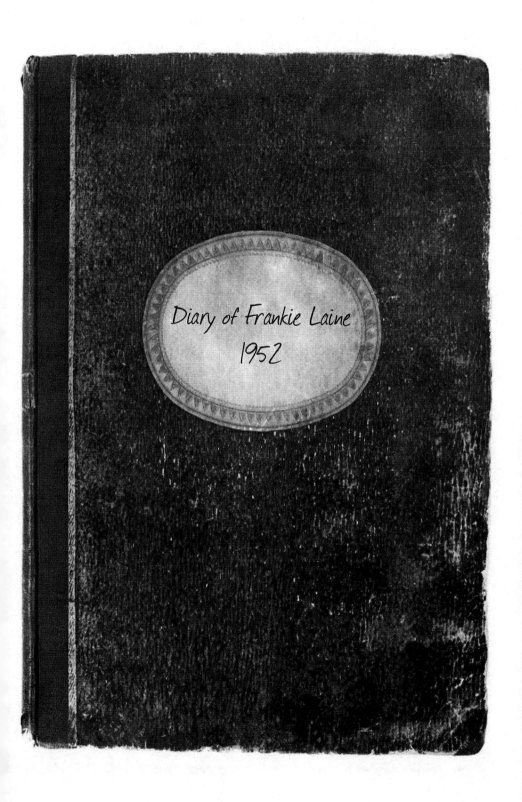

Diary of Frankie Laine
1952

August 12: Left hotel for airport at 2 P.M.
Cress Courtney and Tim Gale threw going
away party at airport We were given presents. Whole thing was touching. Left New
York at 5:32 p.m. and arrived in England
12 hours later. First sight of England awe-
inspiring, inexplicable thrill. Tradition, or
what have you...I don't know...but it was
great!

August 13: Lew Grade met us at London airport, got us through customs, and drove us to
the Savoy Hotel. London is magnificent and
thrilling—what a sight to see! Age, tradition,
history, so many things that make you humble. Nan and I both felt it in a strange and
undefined way.   We checked in and cleaned
up from the trip. The press was very cordial
and met us in the room.   Later, we went on
to a wonderful reception that Val (Parnell)

and Lew (Grade) gave for us at the Prince of Wales Theater. It was quite a thing: we talked and talked and talked for two solid hours, but everybody seemed to think that we did a lot of good. The press bears it out, for our coverage surpassed all other guest stars, or so they told us. At any rate, it was a wonderful feeling, and we had a f ine time doing it. Dinner at the Ward Room - food good-everything up to expectations in every way. Home to bed—too excited to sleep.

August 14: We visited West-minster Abbey, one of the truly exciting and breath-taking events of our trip, so much that the place just def ies description. Then on to

<u>St. Margaret's</u>, all so much beyond anything we knew, that magnificent becomes a puny adjective. Had a charming lunch at Prunier's and then to the <u>Tower of London</u>. Spent the entire afternoon there, but it was insufficient – there is too much to grasp in only one visit: the towers, the bridge, the armories, the stories of each of them, all were amazing. Unfortunately, we missed the crown jewels because of the length of the line and the scarcity of time. Hope we can return; we should. Went to Grenaro's for dinner, afterwards to Clink Street and Old Pub in South London. Saw and felt Whipping Post. On to Club Panama. It's really just a joint, so we

left soon after arriving and walked home through _Picadilly Circus_ and _Trafalgar Square_. Strange feeling. A strange and different place at that hour of the night.

August 15: Started rehearsal. Wolfie Phillips is great. Band is fine. Twelve songs well done in three hours

time. Really made us feel wonderful. Got home at 5:30 p.m. and napped before dinner. Dined at the Albany Club, which is located in what was once Lady Hamilton's residence. Frank Little, the proprietor, is a very nice guy. We all had a grand time.

August 16: Nan and I went to Portobello and Winfield Markets.

Was recognized once in a while by autograph seekers, but all was well until we got to Brady's Antique Shop where a huge crowd gathered and we had to be escorted out by police. Nothing serious happened, only lost a handkerchief, but it was close! Lunched with U.S. Air Force at Winfield House. The nice American prices almost threw us. BBC broadcast at 6:45, then to the Palladium to see Dolores Gray headline a great show. We were seated in the Royal Box and introduced to the audience. Sure felt great.

August 17: Wonderful day. Drive through country. Visit to  Windsor Castle. Saw Neil Gwynn's house, Christopher Wren's crooked home. Wonderful sight seeing, that peculiar feeling that you are walking in the steps of a tradition that is and was greatness itself.

The Opening at the London Palladium:

August 18: Well, today is it—the opening. Rehearsals went smoothly. Wolfie (Wolfie Phillips) did an excellent job. Fanfare from "Desire" is to be my entrance music. At night I stood in the wings of the _Palladium_ while Wolfie introduced me.

What an audience! Great! From the moment I went on I knew I had nothing to worry about. The program was, 1. "So Now We're in London," 2. "Georgia On My Mind,"

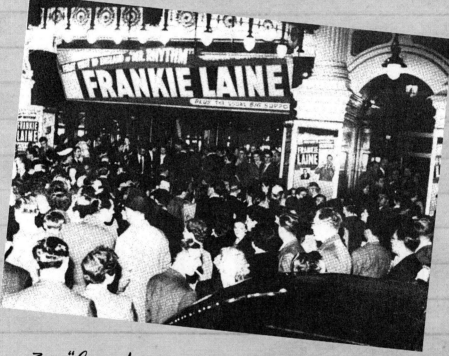

3. "Cry of the Wild Goose,"
4. "That's My Desire," 5. "Jezebel,"
6. "Sunnyside of the Street," 7. "When You're in Love," 8. "Mule Train,"

9. "Lucky Old Sun," 10. "Shine,"
11. "High Noon," 12. "Jalousie." Thanks
and God Save the Queen.

They tell me the reception was greater than
Danny Kaye's. I'm glad, but Carl (Fischer)
and I both know there were greater receptions
in American cities. The phenomenon is that
British audiences are traditionally more
reserved and for them to let loose hysterically
as they did makes the whole thing seem more
than it was, but I'm still grateful. Great ova-
tion in the dressing room after the show-just
wonderful and moving. Second show even
better than the first. Usual first night luck
held with unlooked for accident. In bringing out piano, whole pedal section and one
caster came off. If the critics run true to form,
we should get panned to death. Hope so almost. Will mean that we are a success with
the people, and that's what counts. After

show, climbed up stage entrance ladder and sang eight bars of "Rock," which pleased the fans immensely and got me off the hook with them. Val Parnell threw a big party at the Café de Paris for us. What wonderful people are the Parnells and (Lew) Grades are!

August 19: Notices were as anticipated: by our standards, awful, but according to Val, the (Lou) Grades, and the other British people we were an absolute smash, the biggest attraction to ever play the Palladium.... Hope they're right! SRO lines forming early in morning, so I guess they are right. Anyway, audiences are wonderful, and that's what counts. Went to Albany for supper and met Jose Ferrer who said he was coming to the show tomorrow.

August 20: Up early to see the Horse Guard change at Whitehall. Truly a gorgeous sight.

West to _St. Paul's_.   Most magnificent.
View from the top is worth the trip to London. Performance in evening like opening

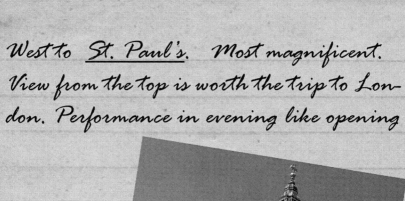

all over again. Made me
feel wonderful. Jose Fer-
rer and Zsa Zsa Gabor
came back after show
and congratulated me.
We all had a drink
at _Les Ambassadeurs_

afterwards. Wonderful place. Used to be Baron Rothchild's home. Zsa Zsa is just wild about "Jezebel," and the band played it for us. Had a long talk with Joe. Wonderful man, truly a genius. I should love to work with him some day.

August 22: More sightseeings, a few good restaurants. Who said the food was rotten in England? Another great audience.

To Blackpool

August 23: The three shows again today. There was very little time to eat so we had to go to a nearby place. The crowd found out where we were and nearly mobbed the Place, dashing in the front and tradesmen entrances. We tried to run for a cab but were spotted, and people leapt in with us. Almost got hurt. It's worse than home, or, should I say, better. Left for Blackpool right after the show with Leslie Grade, who is certainly not the world's best driver. We had a few scares. Arrived at the Clifton Hotel at 4:10 a.m. We've got a nice room with a fine view of the sea.

August 24: Met Katherine Williams, who runs a group of buildings down here. A very nice girl, who showed us around. There seems to be high interest in the show here, and we should do well. After lunch went to rehearsal—a good orchestra, lovely theater, a little bigger than Palladium. The show went very well. The people were as kind as they had been at the Palladium. Carl (Fischer) worked in the pit with the orchestra leader to help the orchestra coordinate the tempos, or should I say, tempi? Second show even better than the first, and I worked up quite a sweat. Left right away through a secret exit, but the crowd found us. We managed to get away though and were back in London by 6: AM.

August 25: Nan spent the day shopping in Brighton, and I just relaxed, recuperating from the

trip. Got to the theater early and signed some pictures. Ray Sonin of Musical Express came to see me. He had given me the best review of my entire career. In the first show I blew the lines of Goose, but it all turned out funny, so it was all right. Second show went better. Took the Sonin's to the Albany Club. Very nice people. He had been the editor of the Melody Maker for twenty-five years before retiring and coming back to the start, the year-old Musical Express, which is building up quite a following.

August 26: Guests of Jose Ferrer for lunch at the studio where we watched some shooting on Moulin Rouge. Jose is magnificent. I think he ought to win a special award, if for nothing else, just for walking on those artificial limbs. His beard gives him a startling resemblance to Toulouse Lautrec. Met John Huston, brilliant director, who, incidentally, is crazy about goose. Joe took us for a spin in his new Jaguar. It's a beauty. Evening shows

MR. RHYTHM

were great. I love playing the Palladium more each time I go out on that stage. Went to Val's (Parnell) for dinner after shows. Grand time. Wonderful people.

Closing Day

August 27: Three shows today, but an absolute pleasure at this theater, and for these tremendously responsive house, I'll hate to see it end. Took the Sam Marx's to dinner at the Les Abassadeurs. When we got home there was a wonderful gift from Jose Ferrer waiting for us.

August 28: Went to Silver Vault. Fantastic place. Did some shopping and went to theater. Excitement still at fever pitch.

August 30: Final performances, but will be

back next year. Everything went beautifully. Blew part of tradition by not introducing the next act - Bob Hope. He hadn't arrived yet, but I read his wire. Vale gave me a book, Top of the Bill, at the Palladium, in which he inscribed that had the book been written today, Carl and I would certainly have a prominent place in it. This was worth the trip in itself. Frank Little gave us a farewell party at the Albany Club. Great Time!

One-Nighter

August 31: Leslie drove us to Leicester. Crowd went wild in spite of bad lighting and only fair orchestra. About 300 people were seated on stage behind me, stomping their feet for applause. Scared Hell out of me. I thought the building was coming down. After second show, back to London, but couldn't sleep. Paris on my mind.

Sept. 1: Left London for Paris. That first view of the city from air is one of the most thrilling sights in the world: the <u>Eiffel Tower</u>, <u>Arc de Triomphe</u> -indescribable. Have a wonderful driver, George, who took us sight seeing before dinner. We're like a couple of kids. Dinner wonderful. Went out on the town afterwards and had great fun.

Sept. 2: More sightseeing. This is the most beautiful city, and the food and wine, wonderful!

Sept. 3: Shopping, sightseeing, dinner with <u>Edith Piaf</u>. Wonderful time. That seems to be all I can say about this trip.

Sept. 4: Finally got to the Louvre. What an overwhelming experience to be surrounded by such a wealth of art and opulence. We were humbled by it.

Sept. 5: Took Nan to <u>Jacques Fath</u> showing. I was bored but she loved it. Jean Auerbach and I left before the end. The girls stuck it out. To the Folies Bergere at night. Spectacular produc-

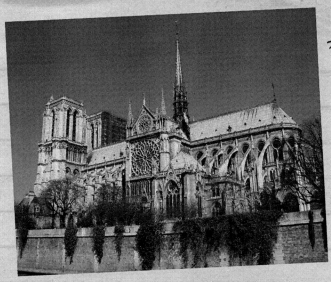

tion, but not much talent. It was like one of our flops at home. An extravaganza with no backbone. Afterwards, to Maxim's. Again, disappointed. The music was blaring.

Sept 6: Notre Dame, Tour D'Argent, Napoleon's Tomb: these awesome European monuments, works of

designing and en-
gineering, genius
tributes to man
and God. Off to
rehearse broadcast.
Used two guitars,
clarinet, bass
and drums. The

broadcast, my first in France, went extremely
well. The program included "Sunnyside of
the Street," "That's My Desire," and "Jezebel." Went to Mme. Salabert's for cocktails
and met Franz Waxman, the musical director and composer from Hollywood. Dinner at
Tour D'Argent.

To Glasgow

Sept. 7: Flew to Glasgow. It was pouring
when we approached it, but view of Scotland
looked lovely. Pilot made a pass at field but

couldn't make it because he had forgotten to let his wheels down. When he did land, a huge crowd broke through the lines and onto the field, and we couldn't get off the plane without police help. When we got to the hotel, <u>all hell broke loose.</u>

There must have been 5,000 people waiting, and we couldn't get out of the car without circling the block a few times and dashing in through the station entrance.

With so many people turning out to greet me, I had to do something, so I climbed out on the marquee and sang "Rock" and "Jezebel." Later there was a party for the press.

Sept. 8: Took some publicity photos and went to rehearsal. It looks as though it will be a wonderful week. The Empire was sold out weeks in advance. The shows went splendidly, even better, if possible, than the Palladium. Harry Lauder's niece, Greta, came back and invited us to tea with the family.

Lauder, a Legend

Sept. 9: Tea with Greta was very nice. The family was wonderfully cordial. What a mark Lauder made on these people. He is almost a legend. Shows went well. Again, shows stopped traffic. It's always heart-warming to see them.

Sept. 10: Nan arrived from Paris today, and it was wonderful having her with me again. We wanted to go out for some sight-seeing, but it is impossible to get through the crowds in the lobby. Matinee today and it was the same beautiful, enthusiastic audience.

Sept. 11: Drove into country for lunch and stopped at <u>Loch Lomand</u>. It was as lovely

as we had been told. Back to theater for show. Another fine house. "When You're in Love" keeps getting better and better. Went to 101 Club for dinner. Owner, Ricci, is a nice guy. His daughter is Adrienne Corri, the girl who was in the film The River, and in June on Broadway.

On the Road Again

Sept. 12: Carl and I had lunch at Screen Stars and Cinema Club where we presented a scroll to the secretary who had given 30 years of meritorious service. The girls went shopping in Edinburgh so we'll probably end up owning the castle. After show, we went to dinner at a private Stage and Screen Actors Club. It turned out to be a sing for your supper deal, but they wanted to hear us, so God bless them.

Sept. 13: Our last day in Glasgow. Nothing very exciting happened. We gave three shows and were escorted to the train by police who have certainly been helpful in getting us through the crowds without anybody getting hurt.

Sept. 14: Arrived in Manchester and went to hotel without much trouble, but when we tried to get to the theater, the car was badly mobbed. The audiences at both shows were great, with SRO sold above capacity. After the show, we left for London directly, with Italy looming very imminently in the future.

In Italy

Sept. 15: We're off at last. Italy. We arrived

at the airport in plenty of time. Stopped at Geneva, an indescribably, beautiful spot. Finally, we arrived at Milano airport. I can't tell you how I felt. A few years ago, I never would have dreamt that I might be able to visit Italy. The drive from the airport to the city is a lone one, but the road was good. Our accommodations seemed small but very adequate to our needs. We went out to dinner at the most magnificent of restaurants, Giannino's.

Now, we let Pop take over. He's the chairman of the Italian tour, and he's in his glory.

Sept. 16: Pio is

our guide, a very nice and amusing little fellow. We went to Santa Maris della Grazie to see Leonardo's Last Supper. Really a great picture; then on to the Breda Gallery. The Louvre had nothing on this. Met Paul Baron's friend Piero Leonardi. We had dinner with him and his

charming wife at their lovely apartment. They have a Giorgioni that knocked us for a loop. Later, we took them out for a drink. The orchestra leader recognized Nan, Carl, and me an began to play "Jezebel." It seems we cannot escape that song.

Sept. 17: First stop was La Scala and the musical museum. Quite a wonderful feeling being in the famous opera house. Then Pio took us through the <u>Cathedral Duomo</u> on the Piazza. In the crypt they have the coffin of San Carlo with his scull in plain view. It gave us a bit of a shock. More sightseeing at the Castello Sforza, also a magnificent museum with a gorgeous Leonardo al Fresco on the ceiling. Picked up the Leonardis took them to dinner.

Sept. 18: Left for Venice by car. The trip through the countryside was really exciting and lovely. When you think about the history of this country and of the people who traveled this same route through the centuries, it leaves you speechless with

wonder. <u>Venice</u> is everything we expected and more. Our rooms at the Lido Isle Hotel are great and give us a gorgeous view of the Adriatic.

Sept. 21: Left Venice for Florence. Luncheon in Farrara. Finally Florence.

Sept. 22: Off to Bellini's Silver place, then to the _Poonte Vecchio_. Visited Danny Quinn's leath establishment. Went to Piero's for dinner with Danny. They insisted I sing "Jezebel." Crowd seem to know it and like it.

Sept. 28: Left Rome via the Appian Way

for Naples.

Sept. 30: Flew to Palermo. It's everything Pop has always said it was. Lovely beyond compare. The city Pop was born in.
Not Frank!

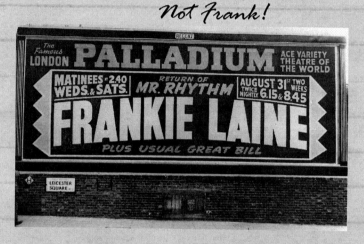

Oct. 1: The heat is unbearable. We would adore this journey if it weren't for the terrible heat. We did some sightseeing and visited the Cathedral. Retired early. Too hot

to sleep. Funny, that after all of these years and all of the talk that we've all indulged in about revisiting Pop's birthplace we should all get ill here. Records show that my great-grandfather, Philip Lo Vecchio, was married to a woman named Salena Sinatra. My great-grandmother.... Sinatra.

Oct. 2: Took boat to Naples. Nan was sick. Met Ella Logan (Editor note: sang lead in original Finian's Rainbow on Broadway) in the lobby. Pop leaving Saturday on Independence. Saying goodbye to him was difficult, but we'll soon be seeing him again.

Oct. 5: Back in London. Never thought it would look so grand to me. Fine night for concert at Tooting. Big Theater, but both shows sold out.

Oct: 27: Well, goodbye to Europe at least for the time being. We fly home today. It'll be great to be home again. Next stop Earle Theater, Philadelphia.

The Blindfold Test

Frankie Flips For

Mr. and Mrs. Laine and friend.

I happened to be at the session when this was made, and to me it was one of the most wonderful things I have ever heard. In fact, when I heard this record being made I was sick that Mitch Miller hadn't given me the song. But as long as I didn't get it I would rather see nobody else get it than Jo Stafford, because she has been one of my favorite people—one of my favorite singers, for quite some time

Jo's 'Jambalaya'

Records Reviewed by Frankie Laine

Frankie was given no information whatever about the records played for him, either before or during the blindfold test.

1. Louis Jordan. *There Goes My Heart* (Decca).
2. Rusty Draper. *Devil Of A Woman* (Mercury).
3. Stan Getz. *The Best Thing For You Is Me* (Roost).
4. Lionel Hampton. *Crying* (MGM). Sonny Parker, vocal.
5. Nat Cole. *You Will Never Grow Old* (Capitol).
6. Joe Costa. *All The Things You Are* (Victor).
7. Woody Herman with Duke Ellington's Ochestra. *Cowboy Rhumba* (Columbia). Quentin Jackson, trombone.
8. Jo Stafford. *Jambalaya* (Columbia).
9. Spade Cooley. *Swingin' The Devil's Dream* (Decca).
10. Joe Bushkin. *If I Had You* (Columbia). Buck Clayton, trumpet; Bushkin, piano.

now.

I love her ideas, I love her voice, I love her trueness and clarity of tone, plus the fact that back in 1947 she was the very first one to ever give me a chance to sing on a major coast to coast program, when she had the Chesterfield Supper Club, and that goes a long way with me, because I have never forgotten that she was the first one to offer me a spot. When we were listening to the playback of this, Jo said she was pretty pleased with the way she had said "Son of a gun!" on the record, because the way I slur things sometimes on records had given the idea to her—which was to me a very wonderful compliment.

You told me not to give any record five stars unless I really flip and this one flipped me on the session. Only one little thing. Some of the listening public might be a little troubled by trying to figure out what some of the words are unless they see it printed. Five stars!

Jo Stafford with husband Paul Weston

Downbeat - October 8, 1952

RAWHIDE

Clint Eastwood and Frankie Laine

A television producer named Bill Doxier needed a song for a new western and went to songwriters Dmitri Tiomkin and Ned Washington, who wrote "High Noon." And told them he needed a song that had to be called "Rawhide," the name of his new show.

In a couple of weeks they had it done. Now they needed a he-man voice to carry the song. They let Frankie Laine listen to it. He loved it and the theme would be played before and after every show.

The song was recorded and did very well but the show almost didn't make it. Sponsors would not stake the money for a show with unknown actors, that included a young Clint Eastwood. Well, they finally got a sponsor and the show, and the song, released for the second time, went to the top.

"For the first four months," said Clint, "the theme song kept the show on the air. People would turn on the show, listen to the theme, then shut it off until the end when they could listen to the theme song again by Frankie Laine during the closing credits."

When Frankie and Nan Laine did a guest shot in 1960, Eric Fleming, Clint, and the rest of the cast all shook Frankie's hand. It was a sincere thank you for keeping them on the air until the show caught on.

RAWHIDE

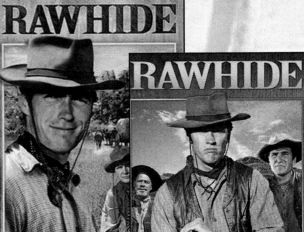

CELEBRITY PAGES

Bob Hope and Hedy Lamarr

with Slugger Ted Williams

with Broderick Crawford

Herb Jeffries "Flamingo" Singer

Frankie, Grace Kelly, Celeste Holm and Frank Sinatra on the set of "High Society"

with The King of England
and Bob Hope

Meeting The King and Queen of England

with Marlon Brando in Paris, 1957

with Tony Martin and Cyd Charisse

Singing for the Soldiers at US Navy Hospital, San Diego

Mr. Rhythm

Hamming it up with
Slim Gaillard

with Patti Page

with Dorothy McGuire and Deborah Kerr at MGM Studio, 1956

with Author Irving Stone and Bandleader Percy Faith

MR. RHYTHM

with Al Lerner, Charlie Shavers and Frank Carrol

At Home in San Diego

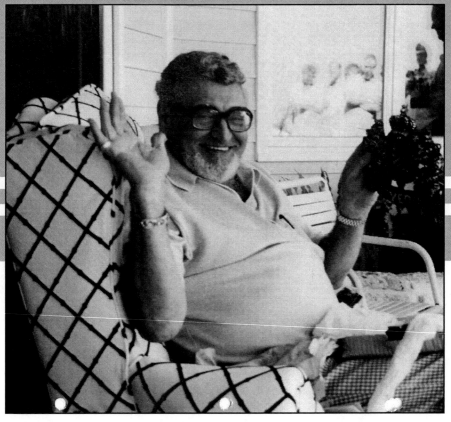

Photography Courtesy Luxury Lifestyles Magazine

Mr. Rhythm

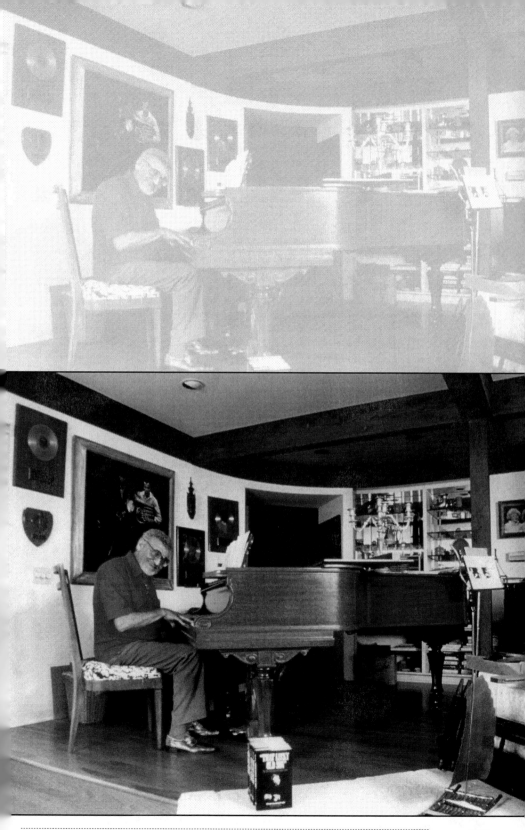

Mr. Rhythm

MR. RHYTHM

SPOTLIGHT ON FRANKIE LAINE

The cream of Frankie Laine's recordings
from the Mercury catalogue,
including the original million sellers

"That's My Desire"
"Mule Train"
"Cry of the Wild Goose"
"Shine"

GARY JAMES INTERVIEW

Courtesy Gary James Interview - www.famousinterview.com

In 1993, Frankie Laine wrote his autobiography titled "That Lucky Old Son." We talked with Frankie Laine a.k.a. "Mr. Rhythm" about a career that's remarkable to say the least.

Q. Mr. Laine, what do you remember about Syracuse and your performance at "Three Rivers Inn?"
A. **Well, the first time we played Syracuse was in a place called Andres. It was wonderful. It opened up the whole eastern coast you might say, 'cause it was one of the first places we played in the New York area.**

Q. How about Three Rivers Inn?
A. **Well, that came later. Dominick (Bruno - Three Rivers Inn owner) was one of the greatest guys I ever met. I played there many times.**

Q. Where else did you perform in Syracuse?
A. **There's a big hall there.**

Q. The War Memorial?
A. **That's it. That's the one. I played there twice.**

Q. Since you've titled your autobiography "That Lucky Old Son," do you feel lucky? Isn't your story more about hard work?
A. **The first 17 years was all hard luck and bad luck. I think it was Jo Stafford who said to me, "you find out after you're in this business long enough that you last just about as long as it took you to get there." (Laughs). Well, it took me 17 years to get there, and I should've lasted 17 years, and I've lasted almost 50.**

Q. I believe you've said that 17 years was a little too long to wait for success; that it should have been half of that.
A. **I would hope so, you know. But, there's only one person that I know of that it took longer and that was Roberta Sherwood. It took her 26 years. But, she had a good excuse. She got married and raised a family. (Laughs).**

Q. So, why did it take you 17 years to be discovered? Were you not seen by the right people in the right places?

A. **Who the hell knows, Gary. I did all the usual things. I think I did everything that everybody else does. I did auditions. I went to see people. I went to see the right people in some instances, the wrong people in others. The wrong time in others. The right time in others. Nothing seemed to make any difference. I quit 5 times! I always went back to try again when circumstances came around to it.**

Q. Do you still perform today?

A. **Oh yeah.**

Q. Where do you perform?

A. **I do mostly one night concerts because the doctors don't want me to travel too much. They don't want me to tour night after night. So when the right place comes along at the right time with the right money and I have a great conductor and I got a good book, we take it. We're doing a big Italian Festival in New Port Richey, Florida. I'm doing a benefit in Scripps Park which is near La Jolla for I guess it's a hospital, I don't even know. It's outdoors and it's in the afternoon. We should be playing Carnegie Hall in the spring.**

Q. How are you able to write songs? Do you play an instrument?

A. **I fool around with guitar and I can fool around on piano. I don't really play either instrument although I can play a couple of songs on guitar. You don't really need to be able to play to compose. There are many composers and arrangers who work out of their heads.**

Q. What do they do, sing it into a tape recorder?

A. **I know people who do that. But, I can usually go to the piano and I can't always get the structural chords, but I can always pick out the melody note I want. Then, if I get the melody note I want for 32 bars, I'll call in my conductor or my arranger and I'll sit down with them and they start trying to figure out the right chords. If they play something that doesn't sound right, I'll say no, and they'll try something else. Finally, we find it. Sometimes it comes quickly, and sometimes it doesn't. But, if it's a good idea and you believe in it, you keep at it, it finally works.**

Q. How did you travel in the early days, was it by bus?

Mr. Rhythm

A. **No. Well, we did a few tours by bus. In Australia, they had limousines. The band would go by bus and the headliners would go by limo, or we'd fly.**

Q. You hear so many rock stars today complaining about how tough the road is as they jet around in their private planes.
A. **Yeah. (Laughs).**

Q. And you and Perry Como and Tony Bennett didn't have the luxury of a private plane and probably didn't stay in a $400 a night hotel room.
A. **That's true. Well, we didn't play ballparks either. You didn't play to 40,000 people most of the time, or 50,000, or 100,000. You can do that when you're playing to that kind of group and charging $20.00 a head, or more.**

Q. Many rock stars will use the excuse of the pressures of the road to explain away their drug addiction.
A. **That's a bunch of b.s.**

Q. Was there less pressure on you and Perry Como and Tony Bennett?
A. **The pressure most of the time is what you make it. If you're gonna go play The White House for the President as compared to playing Paduka, Kentucky, where's the most pressure?**

Q. It's gotta be The White House.
A. **O.K. That's as simple of an explanation as I can give you. The more important the job is, the greater the pressure on the performer, but not the actual touring from town to town - there's no real pressure there, in the sense of a performance. You're doing what you're doing every day. Now, if you're gonna play Paduka, Kentucky and you understand the President is gonna be in the audience, that makes a big difference. (Laughs).**

Q. The grind of touring...
A. **That part of it is unavoidable. It goes with the territory.**

Q. When rock 'n roll became popular in the mid '50's, did you like it or hate it?
A. **I liked parts of it. In every kind of business, in every kind of song, in every section of music, there is always a good song or a bad song. Some songs are crap and some songs aren't.**

Q. Did you like the material that Chuck Berry and Buddy Holly were doing?

A. **I didn't listen too much in the beginning. I was too busy. I thought 'Rock Around The Clock' was a hell of a piece of material for Bill Haley. But, there was a lot of crap that came after that. Most of the guys in the early days of rock could not play the instruments well enough, so everything was at a moderate tempo. There was nobody that played anything that was really up-tempo, or really fast. They couldn't play that fast. Later on when they got better and more expert at it and the better musicians came along who could execute well on the instruments, the songs got better. There was never a better song written than 'Bridge Over Troubled Waters.'**

Q. What a great quartet Led Zeppelin was. Each gig was a master at what he did.

A. **They were absolutely great. Now, everybody thinks The Beatles were a great outfit and they were. But, they were better composers than they were singers.**

Q. I'd challenge you on that one.

A. **The Bee Gees were much better singers.**

Q. The Beatles had their own sound. The Bee Gees had their own sound.

A. **I'm not talking about sound. I'm talking about quality of voice.**

Q. In The Beatles, you had four singers. Every song sounded different than the one before it.

A. **I'll agree with that.**

Q. With The Bee Gees, you can always tell it's The Bee Gees. Their songs sound alike. You can always tell it's them singing. With The Beatles, you were never quite sure, at least in the beginning anyway, who was singing lead.

A. **Yeah. You didn't know who was singing. I agree with you. But, that doesn't necessarily make the quality of the sound great, to me. As far as Paul is concerned, he's a nice left-handed guitar player. He sings pretty well. Can you name 3 singers who sang better than Paul?**

Q. I've always liked John Lennon's voice, but there's no way you're gonna have me pit John against Paul.

A. **Well, there you go. Even within their own group, one guy had a**

MR. RHYTHM

better voice than the other guy.

Q. And together it was a knock-out.

A. **Yeah. I think the best of the three was George Harrison. Musically. Quality sound. He was over-shadowed by the composing ability of the other two guys.**

Q. You saw Elvis in Las Vegas at the New Frontier Hotel in 1956. You said his act didn't go over very well then. Others have written Elvis bombed big time back then. What was his act like?

A. **I think they took him to Vegas too soon. He did his act as he always did it. Had that been a teenage audience, it would've been a smash. But, in those days you didn't get those kids, and they couldn't go in those gambling casinos. So, he had to play to the audience he had, and his act was not geared to an adult audience. His act was geared to his teenage admirers.**

Q. At one point, having left the stage, he came over to your table. What did you guys talk about?

A. **Col. Tom Parker (Elvis' Mgr.) was a friend of mine. He went and got Elvis and brought him to the table. He didn't just come to the table. He sat down with us, me and my wife, and the Colonel. I complimented him on what I saw and what I heard because I could appreciate it. You know, I wasn't 60 or 70 years old at that point. I was 40, 41 years old. I could see his magnetism, his movements. I like a guy that moves. I could see how he tried to communicate with the audience. His vocal quality was never comparable to Perry Como or Tony Bennett. I think there were better rock singers than Elvis but they didn't have all the other things he had. What he said to me was in the nature of a compliment. I said, 'Elvis, this really isn't your audience. You shouldn't feel bad about it, what the response was.' He said, well, if I get to do half as good as you've done Mr. Laine I'll be very happy.' To me that was a great compliment.**

Q. It certainly was. Did you like working in Vegas?

A. **Oh yeah. In those days, Vegas was really a great spot. You could be sure of 4 weeks at one time. Once I played 7 weeks at the Dunes. Once I played 3 months at the Hilton.**

Q. How many nights a week?

A. **Six. When you play the lounge area, you get a night off, which was a blessing.**

Q. Two shows a night?

A. **Three, on weekends. Two shows a night during the week. (Laughs). Your throat really goes haywire. That's why they call it Vegas throat. When that ended I swore I would never do that again. But, that got me the theme song from 'Blazing Saddles' because I was playing Vegas.**

Q. What do you think about today's singers people like Madonna, Michael Jackson?

A. **I like some things. In the early days I liked him (Michael Jackson) better. I think now there's a lot of affectation. It's always better in the beginning when somebody's breaking through. They're hungry, and they're putting out their best. Later on it gets to be more run of the mill. It gets to be old hat, in a lot of instances. I don't know, maybe that's why American audiences are as fickle as they are. In England, once they take you to their hearts, its forever. Over here, the next new guy that comes along is the guy.**

Q. You've got a photo in the book of you and Billie Holiday. What do you remember about her?

A. **Oh, well she was my doll. (Laughs). She was my inspiration from about 1937, or '38, when I went to New York finally. I went to see her at a place on Fifty-First Street. You'll never guess who was playing back-up for her - The Nat "King" Cole Trio. I didn't get to meet Nat that night, but I met her. I complimented her and told her how much a fan I was and so forth. Then, later on, I had a chance to meet her somewhere else and we had a picture taken together. That's one of my pride and joys.**

Q. Your father used to cut Al Capone's hair. Were you ever there when Al Capone walked in the barbershop?

A. **He never walked in. Pa used to have to go to his hotel.**

Q. What did your father tell you about that experience?

A. **Nothing. (Laughs). He kept his mouth shut. He had a horse room in the back of his barbershop, which I never knew was there until long afterwards. We used to go down there. Ma used to take us downtown, four boys, and we all used to get our haircuts. Then, we'd go home. We never knew anything was going on. But, a lot of guys used to walk in, and disappear in the back. I didn't know what the hell they were doing. (Laughs). We were small kids.**

MR. RHYTHM

Q. Don't you wish he had told you?

A. **Yeah. Pa was pretty close-mouthed. All he ever told me was he had to go to the hotel whenever Mr. Capone called. (Laughs).**

Q. It almost seems like performers today need a gimmick to become famous or they have to engage in some shocking behavior. Could a Frankie Laine type singer be successful today?

A. **I have no idea. I really don't know. I will say this; I have seen guys come along with gimmicks and I would say the gimmick is worthwhile if it makes you sing better, or play better. But, if it's just to get attention, then it's doomed to failure in the end, even though it brings you out to the public's attention. If wearing a green hairpiece would make me sing better, I'd wear it. (Laughs).**

LATIN QUARTER FLIPS OVER MR. RHYTHM - FRANKIE LAINE

Robert W. Dana "Tips on Tables" October 14, 1955

"Let's get going, then if you want to flip, it's all right with me," says Mr. Rhythm, Frankie Laine, to those attending his limited engagement as star of "Mademoiselle de Paree" at the Latin Quarter in New York City. Earlier, some startled neophytes, unfamiliar with the antics of Frank Libuse, the mad waiter, flip their lids with genuine anger at the preshow liberties he takes.

Frankie Laine has earned his sobriquet. He leans slightly forward as he sings, as if he were about to battle a stiff wind in Kansas. His hands are always busy, often raised, with the fervor of a revivalist. I'll say he's Mr. Rhythm.

And a consummate showman, too, as he introduces the numbers that have meant much to his career. Because it always was a lucky number for him since he first sang it in 1949, he does "Lucky Old Sun."

GAY! SAUCY! EXCITING!
"Folies Parisienne"

WONDERFUL REVUE

EXQUISITE GIRLS

GRAND FOOD

SHOWS 8 & 12

Lou Walters

LATIN QUARTER

B'WAY AT 48th ST. CI 6-1737

Next comes "Your Cheating Heart," by the late Hank Williams, on whose life a movie will be based; then, nearest and dearest to Frankie's heart, "You're My Desire," then "Jezebel."

By now, as Frankie points out, the audience is really flying, so he introduces his accompanist, Al Lerner, the Cleveland flash, before rushing into his version of "Cry of the Wild Goose." " I Believe" and "Jealousy" wind up a program that should satisfy the singer's fans and win new ones.

MY FAVORITE FRANKIE LAINE MOMENT

TONY COOPER (FLIAS Membership Secretary)

Because Frankie Laine was such a generous star and always happy to meet and talk with his thousands of fans, there are so many memorable moments that it is impossible to write about just one.

with Tony Cooper

One memory I will always treasure was on March 29, 1988. FLIAS had arranged for 100 fans to travel to San Diego for Frankie's 75th Birthday and during the visit we were all invited to visit his wonderful Point Loma Home where Nan provided food and drinks. Fans were allowed to wander about the house snapping precious photos for their albums.

What we didn't know was that on the 29th Frankie had taken over the Gaslight Theater in Downtown San Diego for a special concert just for his fans that had made the trip. This was not his usual concert that featured all the hits but one that featured seventeen numbers he knew his fans wanted to hear. Accompanied by just a small jazz trio he proceeded to amaze us all by adlibbing and singing many of the great jazz songs from his early years and finishing with two songs from his latest album Country Laine.

In August 1988, during Frankie's last tour of the UK, he knew his fans wanted something special so he asked Rosie Carden and me to arrange for him to be booked at the Marlborough Crest Hotel in London so that as many fans as possible could spend a day there talking about their love of his music. He promised that he and Nan would spend a couple of hours with them and answer any questions.

About two-hundred of our members made the journey to London and after the meeting and greeting Frankie and Nan, we arrived to a wonderful round of applause from everyone there. For the next four hours he talked about his career, recordings, stage performances and also answered many, many questions the fans had to ask.

Just when everyone thought he had finished, he took out a backing tape from his latest album New Directions and proceeded to amaze us all by singing six songs from the album while sitting at the table with Nan thus bringing his audience to tears of joy.

As Frankie and Nan prepared to leave they invited Rosie & Ron Carden, George Ramsey, and me to join them at the hotel for a refreshments.

with Pam Cooper

After settling down in the bar we had a long conversation about various favorite recordings that Frankie had made and he was amazed to discover that many fans actually preferred the B side of some of his records. One in particular was "Old Shoes" which had been on the flip of his big hit "In the Beginning." Frankie could not recall the words, however, by coincidence, George had the sheet music with him so Frankie invited us to join him in singing and four very delighted fans had the honor of singing along with Frankie Laine. If only we had remembered to record the event.

There are so many memorable moments I could write about, but that would be a book of it's own.

ANECDOTES

First overdubbing of a song was "Cry of the Wild Goose."

"SINGING IS A CRAFT THAT'S MASTERED BY DOING, WATCHING, PRACTICING, AND LISTENING. YOU CAN'T DELIBERATELY SIT DOWN AND CREATE AN INDIVIDUAL STYLE. JUST DO WHAT FEELS RIGHT TO YOU AND A PERSONAL STYLE WILL EVOLVE NATURALLY OVER TIME. EVERYONE STARTS OUT BEING INFLUENCED BY SOMEBODY ELSE, JUST AS FRANK SINATRA AND JERRY VALE DID, AND JUST AS I DID." - Frankie Laine

Frankie Laine dedicated his autobiography *That Lucky Old Son* that he wrote with Joseph F. Laredo, stating if it wasn't for Carl Fischer, Al Jarvis, and Hoagy Carmichael, he wouldn't have had much of a career to write about. This is proof of his great humility that is so well known.

Did you know that is was Tex Ritter who sang the song "High Noon" as the background for the film of the same name. However, most people think it was Frankie Laine who was singing since it was his recording of the song that sold over a million copies and the version you heard on the radio over and over.

Frankie sang a batch of duets with Columbia artists. Doris Day and Frankie sang "Sugarbush" which earned Gold status. With Jo Stafford it was "In the Cool, Cool, Cool of the Evening," "Pretty Eyed Baby," "Settin' the Woods on Fire," and "Way Down Yonder in New Orleans," and a few others. Jimmy Boyd and Frankie sang "Tell Me a Story," and "Little Boy and the Old Man," among others, too. He also sang with the Four Lads and even John-

with Doris Day

M R . R H Y T H M

nie Ray ("Good Evening Friends") and others.

Doris Day said that besides her recordings with Les Brown, recording with Frankie Laine was a "total joy, and Frankie and I became very good friends."

Holding Up My End of a bargain and Meeting Jean Hancox

I have always experienced joy when communicating with my audiences. When the audience enjoys my appearance, it doubles the joy. You know, no two shows are ever alike. They are live and hard to be exact from one to another.

And, no two audiences are alike. Some ask me how I can stand singing the same songs over and over, night after night, no matter how I feel or how large or small an audience may be.

At every performance I give my all, my best shot. The songs are kept fresh because in the audience there may be those who have never heard me. And you never know who may be out front.

For me, the bottom line is that it's somebody who has put up his probable hard-earned money to see me perform my songs, and that implies a promised commitment on my part. I have made it a distinct habit to hold up my end of the bargain.

I can do no more that give them my very best.

One of Frankie Laine's most cherished memories happened while he was in England during the 1954 tour.

Frankie spent some personal time with a six year old named Jean Hancox, whose both feet were amputated due to an accident and doctor's worried about her recovery. Jean would listen to the radio while recuperating. Her favorite show was Frankie Laine Time.

Frankie received a letter from her and said her favorite song was "Cry of the Wild Goose."

"When I got to Sheffield, I visited young Jean at her home, then brought her to the theater. We played catch in my dressing room. Jean was a brave little kid in a pink dress with a pink ribbon in her hair. Listening to her squealing and giggling and laughing as she ran across the carpet in her artificial limbs chasing a ball, made me as happy as I've ever been in my life."

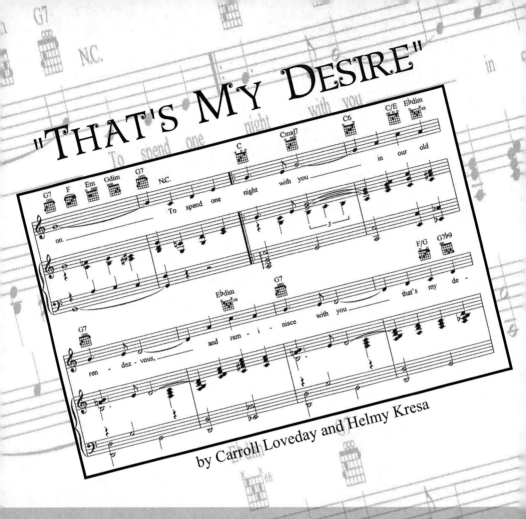

"THAT'S MY DESIRE"

by Carroll Loveday and Helmy Kresa

To spend one night with you
In our old rendezvous
And reminisce with you
That's my desire

To meet where gypsies play
Down in that dim cafe
And dance 'till break of day
That's my desire

We'll sip a little glass of wine
And I'll gaze into your eyes
divine

I'll feel the touch of your lips
Pressing on mine

To hear you whisper low
Just when it's time to go
"Cheri, I love you so"
"You're my desire"

To hear you whisper low
Just when it's time to go
"Cheri, I love you so"
"You're my desire"

You're my desire

ANATOMY OF A SONG

"That's My Desire"

The song, "That's My Desire" is, as we all know, Frankie Laine's first blockbuster recording that landed him firmly on the road to success. There have been many anecdotes about the inspiration and origination of this song.

"Ladies and Gentleman, I have an important announcement to make. I know that I'm just an intermission performer who sings you a few standards to fill the gaps between star attractions here at Billy Berg's. Sometimes you pay attention to me and sometimes you don't. I've been here for quite a while and I've been very content to just sing the same old stuff up until now. Tonight, however, I've got something special for you. Tonight I've got a brand new song… ' That's My Desire'

"With this inauspicious announcement Frankie Laine was now able to jump-start his otherwise fledgling career. From this point he grew into a great, revered singing artist.

The story goes something like this.

Frank: "Back in Cleveland, Ohio, at the College Inn, a girl named June Hart was having her own hard time in her singing career. A friend had told me about her and that she was really very good. My friend asked me to try and help her. There I was needing all the help I could get, but I went to see her anyway and she was very good. She came to my table and I offered to buy her dinner, but she preferred to wait until after her last set.

"She was a fabulous singer, that's for certain. She reminded me of Mildred Bailey. The first Big Band singer. June received tremendous applause. The boss came up to her and offered her a job. She was very happy and I was happy for her. Her salary was to be $35.00 a week, fifteen dollars more than me. When I asked the boss to raise my salary to reach hers, he solved the problem by firing me. He sensed my discontent, I guess.

"That action made June want to quit, but I talked her out of it. After that June allowed me to bunk in with her, on her apartment couch, and we talked and talked about the music. I went to see her perform. The boss could not keep me out. It was a public place. One of the 'oldie's' June would sing was a 1931 ballad entitled 'That's My Desire.'

"I liked the tune and it was kept on a shelf in my head, and maybe in my heart, and it was always on my conscious mind. Meanwhile, Red Norvo was looking for a singer for his band. His girl singer Linda Keene eloped with a band member. I went to see Norvo and told him about June Hart. I told him she sang like Mildred Bailey. Red had been married to Bailey, but was divorced. Red went to hear her, hired her and took her with him to New York. That began my longstanding friendship with Red Norvo, America's greatest vibraphonist.

"'Desire returned to me a thousand fold when I remembered that I liked the song and decided to try it out at Billy Berg's one night when I was shooting the breeze with Edgar Hayes, whose trio The Stardusters were performing at the club. Suddenly, without planning or a lead sheet, I asked Edgar if he remembered the song, 'That's My Desire' "Edgar was about 55 at the time so he remembered it, obscure though the song was to the public and even among musicians."

"Oh yeah, Frankie. That will be a good song for you!"

So "That's My Desire" was re-born and changed Frankie Laine's life dramatically. When he finished singing the place literally erupted and Edgar Hayes was delighted. It took Frankie back to the Merry Garden Ballroom so many hard years ago.

"Frank," said Edgar, "You have a hit on your hands. That's one of the most beautiful songs I ever heard. Sing it again, will ya."

Frank vocalized "That's My Desire" five times that night and a million times since.

Frankie Laine became the headline singer at Billy Berg's, where they had to turn away patrons who came to hear the new sensation - Mr. Frankie Laine!

At first, Mercury Records, led by A & R man Berle Adams, did not wish to record "Desire," but Frankie demanded that if they didn't record "Desire" he would walk out and make no recordings at all. His resolve surprised the management in that Frankie was willing to risk his career for the sake of "Desire" a then practically unknown tune.

When Berle Adams finally read a lead sheet and had the song demonstrated, he changed his mind writing in a telegram, "OK, Frankie! You win. Desire is a great song."

"Desire" was recorded on the morning of September 15, 1946 at the Radio Recorders' Studio on Santa Monica Boulevard in Hollywood. There was me and Carl Fischer, Mannie Klein's All-Stars with Mannie Klein on trumpet, Don Bonne on clarinet, Phil Stevens on bass, George Van Eps on guitar and Lou Singer on drums.

"Desire" was recorded at 9:00AM.

The record was released on December 15th, lost among all the Christmas music that dominated the airways. But, Frank's friend, famed radio disc jockey Al Jarvis played the song just about every hour in the Los Angeles area. As a result of the song's success Billy Berg gave his headline singer a $25.00 a week raise. Billy Berg's was packing them in and Frankie Laine was at last established.

Gratefully for the rest of his life.

TWO LOVES HAVE I

(J'AI DEUX AMOURS)

French Lyrics by
GEO. KOGER and H. VARNA

English Version by
J. P. MURRAY and BARRY TRIVERS

Music by
VINCENT SCOTTO

Recorded by FRANKIE LAINE on Mercury Records

MILLER MUSIC CORPORATION
1619 BROADWAY • NEW YORK

THAT LUCKY OLD SUN

(JUST ROLLS AROUND HEAVEN ALL DAY)

Lyric by
HAVEN GILLESPIE

Music by
BEASLEY SMITH

Recorded by **FRANKIE LAINE on Mercury Records**

Anatomy of a Movie

Rainbow 'Round My Shoulder

Starring Frankie Laine as himself.

Billy Daniels as himself.

Also starring Charlotte Austin, Arthur Franz, and Ida Moore. Barbara Whiting, sister of Margaret Whiting also appears. Their father, Richard Whiting, wrote "She's Funny That Way."

Directed by Richard Quine.

This musical covers the story about a starry-eyed young lady who defies her family and goes to Hollywood. She finds a messenger's job and a big-time studio where she is signed to play in a new film. Her snooty aunt is outraged until the stars of the films, mainly Frankie Laine, offers to appear at the aunt's charity ball.

Songs: "Rainbow 'round My Shoulder"

"Bye, Bye, Blackbird"

"She's Funny That Way."

"Wrap Your Troubles in Dreams."

"The Last Rose of Summer."

 "Girl in the Wood."

"Wonderful, Wasn't It."

"Pink Champagne."

MAKE BELIEVE BALLROOM

Billed as the Hep Parade of 1949, with a lineup of top rhythm musical stars, setting the stage for love and song.

Starring Martin Block of New York's Make Believe Ballroom of WNEW and Al Jarvis of the popular Los Angeles show of the same name, Make Believe Ballroom, originally conceived by Al Jarvis who became a dear friend of Frankie Laine and was instrumental in promoting Laine's early hits, especially his first "That's My Desire."

Al Jarvis plays himself and introduces musical artists Frankie Laine, Kay Starr, Nat "King" Cole Trio, Jack Smith, orchestra leaders Jimmy Dorsey, Ray McKinley, Charlie Barnet, Jan Garber, Gene Krupa, and Pee Wee Hunt, and The Sportsmen Quartet.

Weak Plot: Liza Lee (Ruth Warwick) fast-talking press agent for Al Jarvis, persuades Jarvis to stage a Musical Mystery Contest with a $5,000.00 prize.

Gene Thomas and Josie Marlow are carhops who participate in the Make Believe Ballroom quiz show portion-question and answer of the famous radio series. They tie and share the prize money and together buy the drive-in of their dreams and eventually fall in love. All the musical stars fill most of the picture with singing and performing.

Frankie Laine sings "Sunny Side of the Street." Kay Starr sings "Lonesomest Gal in Town." Jack Smith sings "The Way the Twig is Bent."

The combined orchestras swing into "Joshua Fought the Battle of Jericho" in addition to band alone renditions of many other songs.

The 79-minute film is mostly all music.

SONGWRITING

SONGWRITING - An Avocation of the Love of Music

Frankie put together many sets of lyrics and music to many songs including one with Hoagy Carmichael, something no other popular singer has done before him, that is to collaborate with an established and prolific songwriter like Carmichael. The song was "Put Yourself in My Place."

Frankie also supplied lyrics for "We'll Be Together Again," with Carl Fischer, as well as "I'd Give My Life" "What Could Be Sweeter," "When You're in Love," "The Love of the Roses," all with Carl, and the later a great musical vehicle for Mario Lanza.

Frankie wrote the lyrics to thirty songs with various music composers, including one with the great Duke Ellington, entitled "What Am I Here For," and the last one was entitled "Nan," for which he wrote the music as well.

"We'll Be Together Again" w.m. Frankie Laine, Carl Fischer

"It Only Happens Once" w.m. Frankie Laine

"Put Yourself in My Place, Baby" w.m. Frankie Laine and Hoagy Carmichael

"It Ain't Gonna Be Like That" w.m. Frankie Laine and Mel Torme

"I Haven't the Heart" w.m. Frankie Laine and Matt Dennis

"Magnificent Obsession" w.m. Frankie Laine and Fred Karger

"Torchin'" w.m. Frankie Laine and Al Lerner

"I'd Give My Life" w.m. Frankie Laine and Carl Fischer

"Only If we Love" w.m. Frankie Laine and Al Lerner

MR. RHYTHM

I BELIEVE

Ervin Drake, Irvin Graham, Jimmy Shirl, Al Stillman

I believe for every drop of rain that falls,
A flower grows,
I believe that somewhere in the darkest night,
A candle glows.
I believe for everyone who goes astray,
Someone will come to show the way.
I believe,
I believe.

I believe above the storm the smallest prayer,
Will still be heard.
I believe that someone in the great somewhere,
Hears every word.
Every time I hear a new born baby cry,
Or touch a leaf or see the sky.
Then I know why,
I believe.

Every time I hear a new born baby cry,
Or touch a leaf or see the sky.
Then I know why,
I believe.

I Believe...

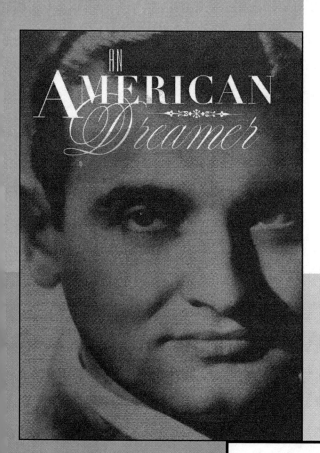

The Frankie Laine
Documentary

A DOCUMENTARY OF THE LEGENDARY SINGER,

FRANKIE LAINE

Frankie Laine: An American Dreamer is a feature length documentary. In this entertaining look at the legendary singer's life, hosted by two-time Grammy Award singer Lou Rawls, Frankie Laine tells his own story in his own words. Classic footage of performances and interviews with esteemed guests as Dick Clark, Ringo Starr, Patti Page, Pat Boone, Maria Cole, Mitch Miller, Michel Legrand, John Williams, Kay Starr, Jack Jones, Herb Jeffries, Peter Marshall, Howard Keel, Terry Moore, Lucy Marlow, Constance Towers, Jerome Courtland, Shecky Greene, Mundell Lowe, Sammy Nestico, A.C. Lyles and Clint Eastwood. From Dick Clark's *American Bandstand* to *The Bob Hope Show,* from *Rawhide* to *Blazing Saddles,* from the *Ed Sullivan Show* to *Gun Fight at the O.K. Corral,* audiences will journey through the life of one of the most popular American male vocalists of all time.

www.frankielaine.com

Approximate Running Time: 2 hours 15 minutes

Executive Producers: James F. Marino and Mary-Jo Coombs
© 2003 JFM International Productions Inc. All rights reserved.

ON THE RADIO, TUBE AND SCREEN

ON the Mike, the Tube and On the Screen: FRANKIE LAINE WAS THERE with HIS VOCAL ACCOMPLISHMENTS

On a show named It's a Great Life, a summer series replacement on Saturday's at 8 P.M. in Hollywood. The cast was Steve Allen, June Foray, Hans Conreid, Frank Nelson and vocalist Nancy Norman and the Wilbur Hatch Orchestra. This was Allen's first network show. He had come to radio as an announcer. His ad-lib talents were obvious and gradually phased out playing records and began impromptu comic routines. Soon people were attending his early-morning broadcasts. He gained further notoriety by winning a bet with Frankie Laine that he, Allen, could write 50 songs a day for a week. As a result, CBGS broadened his base with a new show, "It's a Great Life."

Frankie Laine appeared on television during the 1960s as guests with:
- Perry Mason 1959
- Bachelor Father 1961
- Burke's Law 1963
- And, of course, Rawhide in 1960, with his wife, Nan Grey.

Frank performed on three Academy Award Presentation shows: 1950 singing "Mule Train," 1960 singing "The Hanging Tree," and in 1975 he sang "Blazing Saddles."

Frank's own television shows were The Frankie Laine Hour in 1950, The Frankie Laine Show 1954-55, and Frankie

Frank Lymon & Teenagers on Frankie Laine TV Show, 1956

Laine Time during 1955-56 season. The last was a summer replacement for the famed Arthur Godfrey Show and featured guests Ella Fitzgerald, Johnnie Ray, Duke Ellington, Patti Page, Patty Andrews of the Andrews Sisters, Jack Teagarden, and many others great acts. Connie Haines, who used to sing with Sinatra in the Harry James and Tommy Dorsey orchestras was a regular on Frankie Laine Time and often acted as co-host.

Of course, Frankie appeared as a guest on dozens of television shows from Perry Mason to Burke's Law and on radio, it was, among others, Tallulah Bankhead's "Big Show" on NBC, radio's last stand against the TV giant take over. He also appeared on Bing Crosby's Philco Radio Time and the Chesterfield Supper Club radio show.

HOLLYWOOD

Frankie Laine got in his Hollywood licks too.

Columbia presented six films featuring Frankie Laine. Make Believe Ballroom in 1949, When You're Smiling, a year later, Sunny Side of the Street in 1951, Rainbow 'Round My Shoulder in 1952, Bring Your Smile Along and He Laughed Last. One more for MGM was titled Meet Me in Las Vegas.

Frank vocalized the title song for eight great films.

L-R Harry Zimmerman (Musical Dir.) Duke Goldstone, (Film Dir.) with Frankie and Connie Haines - stars of the "Frankie Laine Show"

- Blowing Wind for Warner Bros. 1953

- A Man Without a Star for Universal in 1955

- Strange Lady in Town for Warner Bros. in 1955

- Gunfight at the O.K. Corral for Paramount in 1957,

- The 3:10 to Yuma for Columbia in 1957

- Bullwhip for Republic in 1958, and

- Blazing Saddles for Warner in 1974.

Frankie Laine's songs have been included in a number of films as part of the soundtrack:

In The Last Picture Show he sang "Rose, Rose, I Love You," my favorite Laine recording. In All This and World War II he sang the Beatles "Maxwell's Silver Hammer." In House Calls he sang " On the Sunny Side of the Street." The vocal "My Little One" in Going Steady in 1980, "That's My Desire" in Raging Bull, "The Love of Loves" in Whore and in Chopper he sang Cole Porter's "Don't Fence Me In" in 2000.

Frank with co-stars in Paint Your Wagon

MR. RHYTHM

TRIBUTES

Comments From Celebrities

JAMES (JIMMY) MARINO - Frankie Laine's Producer

Jimmy Marino and Frankie

How can you describe the experience of knowing and working with a legend like Frankie Laine. As an admirer of this larger-than- life super star, I was truly honored to be his producer. As I worked closely with him, I was able to learn who this giant really was. I saw how he worked, how he cherished his millions of fans. I would see him stay after each concert and make sure that everyone who wanted a picture with him or an autograph, would, for sure, receive their beloved memory of Frankie Laine in person.

In his late eighties, after performing for millions of fans all over the world, he was still surprised that people really liked him. The look on his face when the crowds would cheer and stand up for him, always humbled him. He would say to me, "How'd I do." Of course I'd tell him the truth, they loved you, and they wanted more.

When Mary-Jo Coombs, Frankie's executive assistant, and I produced the documentary, "An American Dreamer" the story of his life, I was amazed to actually interview many superstars who knew and respected Frankie. Celebrities such as John

Jimmy Marino with Clint Eastwood

Williams, Dick Clark, Clint Eastwood, Tom Jones, Ringo Starr, Patti Page, Kay Starr, Mitch Miller, Pat Boone, Michel LeGrand, Howard Keel, Herb Jeffries, Jack Jones, Maria Cole, and Lou Rawls. To each their words were about the tremendous talent their friend, Frankie Laine possessed. When Clint Eastwood, a true legend himself, said to me, "Frankie Laine was a legend to me" I was truly impressed with his humility. Most celebrities had similar warm statements of their relationship with Frankie. I remember Howard Keel saying, "Frankie Laine was one of the best singers of all time."

Frankie Laine was a warm, humble and sweet man. All he ever wanted was to sing his songs. He did that, and did it better then anyone. Working with and knowing Frankie Laine was the true highlight of my life. I was very fortunate to have been so close to the likes of Frank Paul LoVecchio, Mr. Rhythm Frankie Laine.

ANN JILLIAN - Actress, Motivational Speaker

Ann Jillian with Richard Grudens

"I first watched Frankie Laine sing at a NBC network gathering in Burbank many years ago - not only did he sing great but he came off as the world class performer that he truly was. His presence immediately received the undivided attention of everyone in attendance - and those network gatherings are pretty noisy. You could hear a pin drop on his ballad. I didn't get to meet Frankie that night but some years later, my husband and I met him at the San Diego airport where he was meeting his conductor. Frankie could not have been more gracious, truly warm, and down to earth. I felt like I had known him for all my life! I miss Frankie Laine along with millions of his other fans and friends - but I'm confident that he's singing for the good Lord these days in Heaven. Richard Grudens has done such a fine job in his book about Frankie Laine that I think it should be required reading for all of us."

AL JOLSON

The World's Greatest Entertainer said to Al Jarvis, California disc jockey on the original Make Believe Ballroom radio show, and after listening to Frankie Laine's recording of "That's My Desire:" "Hey, that guy is one of the best singers to come down the pike in a long while. He's going to put all of us old-timers out of business."

TONY BENNETT

Al Jolson

"Back in the old days we sold our work live. We went around to record companies to demonstrate the finished compositions by performing them live. Today, you send a 'demo' tape in the mail. One day we tried our luck at the Paramount Theater in New York. Frankie Laine was on the bill with Stan Kenton and his Orchestra, and June Christy was his vocalist. We got backstage and demonstrated the song for them. They all liked it, and Frankie Laine said to me: 'Why are you demonstrating songs? You should be the one making records and singing here on his stage.' "I was floored."

Richard Grudens with Tony Bennett

"Frankie Laine was very kind and encouraging to me when I was scuffling. He was a beautiful person. He really communicated as a singer. He was one of the great popular artists of our time."

MICHAEL FEINSTEIN

Frankie was always enigmatic to me - not as a singer but as a human being, because I had always heard so many different stories about his background that it was hard for me to get a sense of where his unique and singular musical style came from.

He sang unlike anyone else and even though he credited Crosby and others, his voice was truly a distillation of life experiences that were

Michael Feinstein and Richard Grudens

deep and worldly. He didn't sound like he had an easy way with life, but had to earn everything he got along the way.

Sure, he could sing smooth and pretty when he wanted to, but the totality of his journey came out passionately in his work and he went for that passion and unbridled energy over anything too polite, hidden or smooth in his interpretations.

He was also an extremely gifted songwriter and that part of his legacy is still awaiting discovery. He even wrote with Hoagy Carmichael. What other major singer could lay claim to that distinction.

DOWNBEAT POLL 1943
1. Billy Eckstine
2. Frankie Laine
3. Bing Crosby and Mel Torme tied for 3rd.

EDWARD "DUKE" ELLINGTON

Duke Ellington and Duke with Connie Haines and their fans.

From the book "Sweet Man-The Real Duke Ellington" by Don George: The bowling alley building on Vine street in Hollywood might, with a large stretch of the imagination, be called the kid sister of the Brill Building in New York City. It's two stories consisted of a coffee shop and bowling alley on the street level with the upper area being occupied by major music publishers. The Big Three: Robbins, Fiest and Miller, and the like. It was a hangout where songwriters would meet to write and to peddle their tunes. Just north of the building, on Vine Street, was the Club Morocco, which was closed for nonpayment of taxes, throwing the beginning singer Frankie Laine out of work, which situation Duke immediately rectified by talking to Billy Berg and getting Frankie a job in Billy's club by promising to come in a couple of times weekly with a few friends. Billy later helped Frankie with his first record date, which produced "That's My Desire." the record that catapulted Frankie to stardom.

CONNIE HAINES

He had a different sound and he had such emotion and heart. And, of course, you recognized Frankie, just like Sinatra had that sound that you'd always recognize. That's what made for hit records, as well as being a

Jane Russell, Connie Haines and Beryl Davis

great singer. But you have to have a real special sound that never changes. He could do it all...but again, you always knew it was Frankie Laine. I loved being on his show and listening and watching, and singing with him, too.

RHONDA FLEMING

Dear Richard, I received your questionnaire regarding Frankie Laine. I will tell you that Frankie Laine sang the intro

Rhonda Fleming

song for one of my western films and, of course, it was great. I loved the deep, rich sound of his voice. He was an incredible talent.

In reading Frankie's quote regarding Bing Crosby, it would seem that we were both hugely impacted by Bing's singing style - as you know, I sang with Bing in the film A Connecticut Yankee in King Arthur's Court and I well recall Bing 'coaching' me as I sang in my trained soprano voice to sing down an octave - which was very foreign to me, but the outcome speaks for itself when listening to the songs we performed together in the film, which worked beautifully.

I am grateful for this book about my dear friend Frankie Laine and I send my warmest wishes for its great success.

JEANNE MARTIN - FORMER MRS. DEAN MARTIN

Dean and Jeanne Martin

To address my link to Frankie Laine - I have never forgotten this:

In high school in Coral Gables, Florida, while all my friends were 'swooning' over a new singer - Frank Sinatra and "All or Nothing at All" I was on my little radio listening to Sarah Vaughan singing "A Hundred Years from To-day" - "Sunday Kind of Love," etc - - that exact genre. Then I heard "Black and Blue" - if he did not record that - it was a song in that genre - a white man singing their story. That was Frankie Laine.

And it has never left my memory that a white, famous man would feel that need. I hope you get my 'drift' here.

So sincerely yours, Jeanne.

STAN BALL - AL JOLSON SOCIETY, U.K.

As a teenager, in the early 1950s, I was abso-lutely infatuated with most of the pop stars of that era and I played their music constantly and repeatedly. This was the age of vinyl records the 33 1/ 3 rpm long-play-ing discs and with single tunes on 7 inch 45 rpm discs. I had already become an ardent fan of Al Jolson, since

Stan Ball

the age of just 11 years, a devotion which was to stay with me all my life and is still with me some 60 years later. These newer stars back in the 1950s, however, were something else and though I found I enjoyed the music of the likes of Johnnie Ray, Guy Mitchell, Jo Stafford and the like, one name seemed to shine out above all the rest - and that was the one and only Frankie Laine.

His records from "I Believe" to "Answer Me" to "Rawhide" to "Sunny Side of the Street" along with many others, dominated my teen-age years. This devotion to the music and voice of Frankie Laine went with me when I joined the Royal Air Force in 1954 at the age of 18 years. Apart from my full-time day job serving Queen and country, I became a disc-jockey on the camp radio station broadcasting most evenings to over 1,000 Air Force personnel, at St. Eval in North Cornwall, England, where Frankie Laine's records were probably the most requested tunes during my 3 year stint working on the radio station.

Never in my wildest dreams, did I ever imagine, at that time, that in the 1970s, I would make contact with Mr. Laine, when I sent him my very first fan letter. The response I received was so full of warmth that it seemed to have come not from the superstar that I had long-admired from afar, but more from a close friend that I had known and been in touch with for years. I realized then, that this was a man who was a wonderful singer and entertainer, but also a very caring and kind individual who probably loved each and every one of his admiring fans as much as they certainly loved him. Over some three decades or more I continued to exchange correspondence with him, first by what is now termed "snail-mail" and then ultimately by computer using electronic mail. Even though with this advancement, I regularly exchanged hand-written notes, letters birthday and Christmas cards, by post and still retain many of these to this day. My status as one of his fans quickly changed and we both considered each other as just good friends, something I cherish to this day.

One of my most poignant memories is a letter he wrote to me, which regrettably I seem to have mislaid, in response to my condolences sent to him at the time of the death of his then wife Nan (Grey). His letter went into great detail about how he and Nan had been relaxing on the balcony overlooking San Diego Bay when she said she felt unwell. De-spite his repeated pleas, she refused to let him call a doctor to examine her, but eventually he was so concerned, he left her and went inside to phone for his medical adviser. He was only gone a few minutes, but when he returned to his wife, she was dead. He confided in me of his anguish at that time and also how he eventually scattered his wife's ashes, from their boat into the waters of San Diego Bay, because of the wonderful times they had spent afloat in that region. This, I think was the point at which I realized that this man was no longer the superstar that I had long admired from afar as just another fan of his, but someone who regarded me as a true and loyal friend that he could confide in with his innermost thoughts and feelings at such a traumatic time in his life. Although I have mislaid that letter I clearly remember the content and I do still have the memorial card for the passing of his beloved Nan Grey. I also cherish a copy of a video, later converted to DVD of Frankie performing in November 1999 at the Orleans Hotel & Casino, Las Vegas when he was just 87 years YOUNG and although he was in the twilight of his life you can still see that he had not forgotten how to put over a song to captivate, entertain and enthrall his audience. This DVD also contains some footage of him, relaxing at home with his beloved wife, Marcia, and his dog once again showing the true and caring nature of this remarkable man.

I am very proud to include myself among his many fans .

God Bless you Frankie - a little part of all of us died with you and the world is a much sadder place since your passing.

TONY BABINO (TONY B)

One night, several years ago, I logged onto the internet to check my email, and to my disbelief I had received a message from Frankie

Tony Babino (www.TonyB.org)

Laine. The message contained well wishes for my having been included in Richard Grudens' newest book The Italian Crooners Bedside Companion, for which he had written the introduction. Mr. Laine wrote that he had heard and read a lot of wonderful things about me, and that he wished me all the best for a long and successful career.

Receiving and reading that message remains a special moment in my life. When a legend like Frankie Laine, who was one of my own idols, personally writes to you, well, what can I say except it was a humbling and unforgettable experience. Being a person who loves the music and its history, I consider it an honor to speak to, or hear from, the great singers and songwriters who actually created the Great American Songbook. Over the years, I've had that opportunity several times, having met both Tony Bennett and Margaret Whiting. One of my greatest thrills of course, was having worked with the great Connie Haines for nearly ten years. Everything I know about live stage performing, I learned from watching her. She was incredible, and was one of the swingingest singers of all time. One of my regrets is that, although I saw Frank Sinatra and Sammy Davis Jr. perform many times, I never had the pleasure of meeting them.

Frankie Laine was one of those unique singers who I call a musical chameleon who could virtually sing any kind of song, in almost any genre, and perform it validly. Like the great Al Jolson, Frankie had a huge voice and could fill any theatre without the use of a microphone. His nicknames, including Mr. Rhythm and Mr. Steel Tonsils, bear that out. Frankie always stated that Al Jolson was one of his idols, and that it was seeing Jolson perform that made him want to be a singer. Being a fan of Al Jolson myself, I can attest that hearing that Jolson voice had the same affect on me. Frankie Laine and Al Jolson had much in common as vocalists. They were both belters and were influenced by Black music….and their unique voices are easy to recognize. Legend has it that Jolson wanted Laine to portray him in *The Jolson Story*, and when he and Frankie met on a movie set of *Jolson Sings Again* in 1949, Jolie remarked that Frankie Laine was "…going to put all of the other singers out of business". That quote is nothing short of incredible coming from the man who was called The World's Greatest Entertainer…. and is a testament to Frankie's incomparable talent, and how highly he was regarded in the business.

Frankie Laine's body of work speaks for itself. With 20 Gold Records, 6 dozen charted records, and over 100 million records sold, he remains one of the all-time greats. The current generation, unfamiliar with his fame, may not realize they have heard his voice in classic movies like *3:10 to Yuma, Gunfight at the OK Corral, Blazing Saddles, and Raging Bull*, and on television in *Rawhide* with his friend Clint Eastwood. But, people always knew it was him when the first notes punctuated the big screen. Frankie was also an accomplished songwriter, having written lyrics with Mel Torme, Matt Dennis, Carl Fischer, and Hoagy Carmichael, to mention a few.

First time I heard that magnificent voice was when I was a kid thumbing through my grandparents record cabinet. The song was "I Believe." I became a fan forever. When I listen to that recording today, I am still blown away by how incredible and unmatched it remains. Thanks, Frankie for all of the great music and the inspiration.

MARY-JO COOMBS

Mary-Jo Coombs

What an honor it was to work alongside the legendary Frankie Laine as his Executive Assistant. I found the onstage man was as warm and thoughtful as the man who performed before thousands of his adoring fans. We constantly received messages from all over the world, fans sending their love and words of adoration to their favorite singer. I was in the enviable position of communicating with these enthusiastic admirers I learned firsthand how he touched their lives. His music was tied to their most cherished memories. Frankie Laine was indeed larger than life. We continue to receive fan mail as there was a distinct contrast between the exciting performer and the inspiring, creative boss and friend I knew daily at work.

My years with Frankie Laine remain a memorable, once-in-a-lifetime experience.

ERVIN DRAKE -Composer and Lyricist, Television Producer

Three great singers improved my life: Frank Sinatra, Frankie Laine and Billie Holiday. They made the seminal recordings of "It Was a Very Good Year." "I Believe," and "Good Morning Heartache." But none of

Ervin Drake and Richard Grudens
Five Towns Music College - 2008

them were as personally close to me as Frankie Laine with whom I worked on a television series. Nor was any artist of my lifetime as much a regular guy as Laine. He was never aloof, always the same sweet feller. Of them all, I miss him most.

I remember Jimmy Shirl and I were co-writers of the Frankie Laine series on TV. So we saw a lot of him. We pushed his record releases by programming them on the CBS shows.

The wonderful man is gone from our midst and yet we

still speak of him often. Why? Because he was the sweetest man and performer to ever pass our way. A great singing star who was totally unaffected. How many others have you known? It is a rarity.

I have always been thrilled by his rendition of my "I Believe." No one ever sang it better or more sincerely. My co-writers, Irvin Graham, Jimmy Shirl, and Al Stillman heartily agreed.

JOE FRANKLIN

Frankie and Nan Laine and I go way back to the time we all had dinner one night with Paul Whiteman, who was known as the *King of Jazz*. I was working for Whiteman as his record-picker, much like I did

Joe Franklin - Al Jolson Conference

with Martin Block at WNEW a few years earlier. Whiteman had a show called the *ABC Radio Record Club* and was great fan of Frankie Laine and Patti Page. It was the first DJ show to go national on the networks.

During conversations Nan would say something like, "Oh, most of my movies were 'B' movies." Then Frankie would fiercely retort; "Well, they may have been 'B' to you, but to me they were all 'A's.'" They really loved one another.

Whiteman would say, *"Let's go to Memory Lane* with Frankie Laine" then play all his top hits while Frankie sat across the mike from him. I always made sure his records were available for Whiteman to play.

Everyone loved Frankie Laine. He was kind, talented and a great friend. He was on my own show many times and we always enjoyed his visits and always brought his beautiful wife, Nan. I really believe that Nan Grey Laine was one of the top ten beauties on the screen. I guess she gave it all up to be with Frankie. They had a good life together.

JULIUS LA ROSA

Julius La Rosa

Richard, thanks for the opportunity to express my thoughts and recollections about Frankie Laine. First, I've always loved his given name, LoVecchio!

It all started at Grove Cleveland High School in Ridgewood, Queens, New York: the Friday night dances. This is 1947. To "That's My Desire," my high school sweetheart and I would fox trot around enjoying,…"Cherie, I love you so…" Fast forward to the mid '50s, I was the new kid on the block with a lot to learn, and I get to meet him. I'd not yet learned how to walk on stage, and meeting him was a rather exciting moment. He couldn't have been warmer and friendlier.

Through the years we'd run into each other, and each time was a pleasant and enjoyable encounter. A unique style and sound, whether in a ballad or a rhythm song there was no mistaking who was singing! Frankie Laine was truly 'ONE OF A KIND"!

JERRY VALE

I first met Frankie Laine in the mid-fifties. He was a very instrumental influence early in my career. A very caring man, totally unselfish with his wisdom and knowledge about how to manage our careers in the very competitive business we were immersed within. For all the years we knew one another, he was a good friend for all my professional life. I will treasure his memory always and will never forget his unique music, style and ability on the

Jerry Vale and Richard Grudens

worlds' great stages. God bless you Frankie Laine.

SYBIL JASON - Warner Bros. Kid Star

Around 1948 my husband Tony and I took in a little nightclub on Vine Street and heard a singer by the name of "Devecchio" or something

Sybil Jason with Al Jolson, Sybil and her Husband Tony with Tony Babino

like that. We were so impressed with his voice and personality we went back the next night and were sure that that man would become a star if anyone had the wisdom and taste to sign him up and give him a break. Five years ago there was a place that was a second Schwabs drugstore but located in Studio City in the coffee shop of the Sportsmens Lodge Hotel. Every Saturday morning we would all meet for breakfast and the customers were a potpourri of great talent. On the walls were framed memorabilia that a lot of us donated to the coffee shop. Marion Ross and I had our own corner that we shared. Mine was a duplicate and blow-nup poster of a movie that...Lord Bless us, I was billed over Bogie called "The Great O'Malley" and Marion donated her jacket from her popular TV series. One Saturday, after the Jolson Society had featured Frankie Laine and myself in their journal, who should turn up but Mr. Laine himself and we shared a booth and some memories. What a delightful man. He had lost a lot of weight and was sporting a beard then but his enthusiasm was the same as when Tony and I had enjoyed Mr. Lo Vecchio in 1948!!!!!! I am so glad I finally got to meet him and that he had attained his rightful place under the sun!

MARIA COLE (Mrs. Nat "King" Cole)

Most of my relationship with Frankie was through my husband who Frankie respected and adored. However, I am happy to say our

Nat "King" Cole

closeness remained for sometime after Nat's passing when he and Nan (his wife at the time) and I lived nearby each other in Malibu.

Also, it remains to say that although Nat's television show in 1957 was short-lived…although he

Maria Cole

had lots of support with people like Frankie Laine, who was, I believe, the first white entertainer to appear on his show. There followed many others. That sealed the friendship between Nat and Frankie. When Nat passed away in 1965 I gave Frankie a money clip that was Nat's as a remembrance of their friendship. Much luck with the tribute.

MAX WIRZ - Swiss Broadcaster Radio Eviva

The first time I became aware of Frankie Laine was during the winter of 1946-1947. I lived in Kreuzlingen, Switzerland on Lake Constance. I was twelve and had my first English lessons in school and was regularly listening to the American Forces Network with studios in Frankfurt, Stuttgart and Munich. Although I was just beginning to read, speak and understand English I was eager to take in all those wonderful programs like: "People are Funny with Art Linkletter," "Amos and Andy," "Fibber McGee and Molly" even "The News compiled by AP, UP, and INS." And of course I enjoyed the music programs "Luncheon in Munchen," "Arthur Godfrey's Talent Scouts," "Your Hit Parade" and "There's Music in the Air." The voices of the announcers were music to my ears and I adapted the American way of speaking English much to the disdain of my

English teacher. These were programs and sounds we could not hear on Swiss National Radio.

Then one day a song and a voice hit me. "That's My Desire" sung by Frankie Laine, a name I had not heard before. The song was soon repeated day in, day out so that I was able to copy down the words and sing along with my first Singing Her. Then other songs followed: "On the Sunny Side of the Street," "That Lucky Old Sun." In 1949, when "Mule Train" came out I was fifteen and an eager freestyle swimmer. After practice I would sing "Mule Train" in the shower and me and my buddies would slap our wet chests with our hands to mark the whip crack. (Decades later I learned from Frank that for the recording, Mitch Miller had the sound engineers slap two "two by fours" together.)

In 1954, I immigrated to the United States. For my 20th birthday my boss and sponsor gave me a small radio on which I could listen to the New York stations, especially to WPAT. Then in 1955, Frankie brought out

Frankie Laine with Max Wirz at Frankie's home in San Diego, CA

"Hawkeye" - They call me Hawkeye 'cause I can spot a pretty chick a mile away. To this day, that song never left my mind. However, I never was able to secure a copy of it. In 1957, I was drafted into the Army and was stationed in Germany, where I could listen again to AFN stations. The years flew by. My professional career then brought my family and me back to Switzerland in 1970. Unfortunately AFN stations had reduced their radius and Swiss National Radio was more into Swiss Folklore rather than American Songs and Swing.

In 1986, I had the opportunity to produce and present a two hour music program on our local radio station RADIO THURGAU . I started with 30 LPs and added more music, among them songs by Frankie Laine. I wanted to include "Hawkeye" in one of the programs, but I couldn't I find that song anywhere. Then I met Frank Touhey of Cheltenham, England, a recording business associate of Ray Anthony. Frank suggested that I get in contact with Rosemary Carden, President of the Frankie Laine Appreciation Society of England. I did write to Rosemary and she sent me a tape with "Hawkeye" on it.

In the early '90s, while on a vacation trip to California and San Diego, residents Linda and Frank Brennan suggested I interview resident Frankie Laine. While the idea sounded great, I was not so sure that a great American Star of radio, stage, screen and TV was just waiting for Max Wirz of Swiss RADIO THURGAU to spend time for an interview. Linda insisted and later called Frankie Laine who answered: "Tell Max to call me when he is again in San Diego!" Meanwhile, I sent Frank music cassettes of my programs in which I played his songs and we became "pen pals." During the fall of 1996 we again included San Diego in our vacation itinerary and I did call. Nelly and I met my "Singing Hero" at last. Frank was waiting for us in the driveway of his home on Point Loma, high above San Diego Bay across from the Coronado Hotel where we stayed. He greeted us as though we had known each other for years. We took photos, which I destroyed inadvertently when removing the film. During a two hour interview Frank told me the story of his life. I mentioned how I got struck by "That's My Desire" and his voice when I still was in knee pants. During the interview, I read Frank the introduction which I had prepared and which I would use in my show: "Today we are proud and privileged to visit with one of the great American Entertainers of the past 50 years. Mr. Frankie Laine, welcome to RADIO TURGAU. Frankie Laine's personality and voice made him one of the creators of the popular radio, television and film music of the 40's right up into the 80's and into the 90's. Frankie Laine to me is a Jazz singer, a crooner, balladeer and country Preacher. He is a Western hero, at times a belter of songs and in recent years a compassionate benefactor for the sick and the underprivileged." Frank seemed flattered, but he flattered me even more when he replied: "That's a hell of an introduction, I really appreciate it, Max". On the way to lunch, much to our surprise he put a play back tape into the deck and sang "Ol' Man Jazz" live especially for Nelly.

The next evening, Frank Brennan cooked for Marcia, Frank, Nelly and I. The dessert was Swiss semi -soft cheese named Arenenberger, bought at Strähl's, makers of fine cheese in Siegershausen, Switzerland. It was served with red Bartlett pears. Frank's reaction to that delicacy was: "My doctor forbade me to eat cheese and such. But this is so damned good! Can I have another helping?"

In the summer of 2004 we took our son and family for a visit to California and had a second opportunity to meet Frank and Marcia, by now Mrs. LoVecchio. Again we met at the house way above San Diego Bay and I had a chance to have another photo taken with my "Singing Hero". Later we relocated to "Po Pazzos" for Lunch. As Frank was recuperating from surgery, we abstained from a further interview and simply

MR. RHYTHM

spent time visiting and exchanging stories. We kept in touch by telephone and mail until Frank passed away in February 2007.

Of all the interviews I have recorded with American and European celebrities and entertainers, the one with Frankie Laine, including our second meeting with him, will remain highlights with us for as long as we live. I don't think that I have met a more humble and gentle person in my entire life. Most likely "Hawkeye" is up there keeping a watchful eye on us.

Thank you, Frank for your friendship and kindness.

DON KENNEDY - Big Band Jump Radio

Two events come to mind when I think of Frankie Laine. One is the interview I had with him shortly following the release of "That's My Desire," the recording that brought him to the attention of a broad segment of the public. I was a college kid announcing at night at WBVP in Beaver Falls, Pennsylvania. On my own time, in order to enhance the record programs I did at night, I would drive the thirty miles to Pittsburgh to interview top stars appearing in clubs and ballrooms in the city, and often at Pittsburgh's Stanley Theater. We were in his dressing room in the wings while the movie's muted sound was seeping through the door.

Don Kennedy

Frankie Laine was dressed in his robe relaxing between shows and this half-century later I recall his answer to my question about style. He said, "If you haven't lived in the blues, you can't sing the blues."

My second experience involving Frankie Laine was a few years later when I was fortunate to be in Los Angeles on vacation and was invited to watch legendary announcer Al Jarvis do his afternoon program on KFWB, then owned and with studios on the Warner Bros. lot. It so happened that day he was introducing a song by Frankie Laine never before heard. It was a pre-release copy of the Mercury recording of Mule Train complete with simulated whip cracks and looping rhythm. I later discovered Frankie Laine and Al Jarvis were good friends, enabling Jarvis to get the jump on everyone else with an early copy of the recording. As you can imagine, a few days later when "Mule Train" was released it was made a part of the program "Don of Rhythm," hosted by me every night at ten o'clock.

The overriding memory I have from that one meeting with Frankie Laine and the stories written about him since can probably be summed up with the word "intense." He seemed to me to be highly focused with a strong drive to succeed, and succeed he did on both a professional and a human level. He lives on as a standard bearer of that era.

AL LERNER - Composer, arranger and Consummate Musician

Frank and I first met in Cleveland, both working little joints. We worked for almost nothing. Consider this story about how Frank let people down kindly and lightly: A fellow walked into the dressing room and asked Frank, "Are you Italian? I'm Italian too! I got kids, and, you know if you make a record, the kids could get some money."
Frank said , "Let's hear the song."

The song was, and I am being generous, very amateurish and un-professional. Frank said to him, "let me play you a song that Mitch Miller turned down, and this was written by a well-known writer. Do you think your song is as good as this one?"

Al Lerner

The would-be songwriter, incredible as it seemed, said, "Frank you and me we're Italian. I got a couple of kids. You put my song on record…well, you know what I mean."

Frank sat quietly for a moment and looked intently into the man's eyes and said, "If one of your kids had appendicitis would you let me operate on him?"

The man's eyes widened and he said, "Frank, you ain't no doctor."
"That' right," Frank said," and you're not a songwriter and I won't put my life in your hands either." Frank could really handle people with style. Then I became the pianist who took the place of Frank's longtime pianist and conductor Carl Fischer. Patty Andrews had told me of Carl's passing and that they were interested in me. I traveled with Frankie Laine to a Command Performance in Europe to play for the Queen of England. Frankie Laine and I experienced much musical miles and great fellowship

together for a number of years. That included tours of Europe and Australia and every day was a great day working with the wonderful Frankie Laine.

I'd have to say it was always a great experience no matter what the situation.

BOB DOLFI - Lanzalegend.com

A Brief Moment with Frankie Laine

I met Frankie Laine at the Mario Lanza ball in Philadelphia where he sang for us around 1966- 1967. I had the opportunity to sit and talk with him a few times and of course Mario Lanza's name always came up.

We spoke about a song that Frankie Laine wrote and Mario Lanza sang which was "When you're in Love."

I (tongue in cheek) asked him his opinion as to how he liked Mario Lanza's rendition? His answer really surprised me when he said; "Mario Lanza sang it better than anyone else and there will never be a better rendition than his." He went on to say how Mario changed the way people viewed opera and for that matter, singers in general. He basically ended this conversation by saying Mario Lanza had the ability to mould a song into his heart and released it with his voice!

Bob Dolfi

We discussed Mario's voice and songs in further detail but I will always remember that one statement Frankie gave me. In parting, Frankie said to me that the world is much poorer with the passing of Mario as Mario Lanza brought much of the world together through his music.

Because of this statement Frankie made, and if you visit my web site lanzalegend.com - you will see the caption that says: "Mario Lanza Brings Good People Together." I changed his saying a touch but it actually came from Frankie Laine's very own words.

KAREN LAKE - Author

At the age of ten, I discovered the great music I have since cherished through the years. One of the greats was Frankie Laine. He was a gifted singer and songwriter, his songs taking us back to those wonderful years when life was a little easier and less hectic. I treasured his brilliant style, his warm personality and that wide smile on his face, so contagious.

The love songs he sang are a gift to be treasured by us all. Always to be remembered are his great contributions, and the admiration of his friends, family and fans as one of the genuinely nice performers.

Most of his recordings fall into the pop category of songs: "My Woman, My Woman, My Wife" was one of my favorites as was "Jezebel." Frankie Laine has a most unforgettable voice. I suppose all of these beautiful songs have influenced me as a songwriter and composer, though at the time I didn't realize I would be writing songs myself, as it simply evolved because Frankie, through his voice and songs was a great teacher and solid influ-

Karen Lake

ence. When I listened to him I listened with my heart and soul. I try to feel what the performer feels when he is singing and I truly believe Frankie Laine sang from the heart. Frankie Laine's music lives on for us and future generations. God Bless Frankie Laine.

HERB JEFFRIES - Duke Ellington "Flamingo"
Vocalist

You can't categorize Frankie Laine. He's one of those singers that's not in one track. And yet, and still I think that his records had more excitement and life into it than almost anyone including Jolson. And I think that was his big selling point, that he was so full of energy. You know when you hear his records it was dynamite energy.

Herb Jeffries

PATTI PAGE

I think that Frank was probably one of the forerunners of blues and of rock 'n' roll. A lot of singers who sing with a passionate demeanor-Frank was that. I always used to mimic him with "That's

Patti Page

My Desire." And then Johnnie Ray came along and made all of those kind of movements, but Frank had already done them.

JOHN WILLIAMS

John Williams

Frankie Laine was somebody that everybody knew. He was kind of a household word like Frank Sinatra or Bobby Darin or Peggy Lee or Ella Fitzgerald -- Frankie Laine was one of the great popular singers and stylists of that time. ... And his style ... he was one of those artists who had such a unique stamp -- nobody sounded like he did. You could hear two notes and you knew who it was and you were right on the beam with it right away. And of course that defines a successful popular artist, at least at that time. These people were all uniquely individual and Frank was on the front rank of those people in his appeal to the public and his success and certainly in his identifiability.

WILL JORDAN - Master Impressionist

Will Jordan

I have worked with Frankie Laine several times...at the Casino Theater in Toronto, the Nugget Club in Sparks (near Reno) Nevada, and on the Ed Sullivan Show. He asked me to tell Sullivan that he would be glad to replace him on the Sunday Night show...as if I had the power to influence Sullivan. One night he popped up behind me when I was imitating him and sang with me.

CRISTINA FONTANELLI

Cristina Fontanelli

My Frankie Laine story: During one of the very first appearances I ever made was at the Festival Italiana. Afterwards there was a party in a lovely little house on the grounds. There I had the opportunity to meet and speak to Frankie Laine. I was so shy then. He was wonderful, kind and polite and did everything to place me at ease. I marveled at his wonderful singing. He explained to me he had studied operatically as a young man and there he learned breath control. He wanted to sing opera, but didn't continue to study, because he couldn't afford it. When I sang with Sergio Franchi, he told me he converted to popular singing for the same reason and he also became tired of "starving." I think that's why I followed along the same road. However, my story is different because I still have my foot in the operatic door, so to speak. Well, we'll see what happens.

VAN ALEXANDER

There are two things that come to mind whenever I think of my old friend Frankie Laine. They are taste and class. These things can't be acquired, you either have them or you don't. Frank had good taste in selecting his recorded material and had style and class in the way he lived his life. I remember one time when his pianist, arranger and conductor for more than twenty years, Ray Barr, fell ill with a brain tumor. Myself and a few other friends promoted a tribute benefit to help with the tremendous bills Ray incurred. Frankie Laine was first to agree to sing for Ray, along with Martha Raye, Kay Starr and Les Brown with his band. It was held at the Hollywood Palladium . It was a sellout and we turned all the proceeds over to Ray and Betty Barr. This was just one of many instances when Frankie was willing and ready to help someone in need.

Van Alexander

It demonstrated what a class act he was. I miss him dearly, but what a grand legacy he left for the entire world to be able to hear his recorded voice singing his many hits. I'm sure he's singing and entertaining "up there" acquiring new friends and fans. Until we meet again old friend, keep swinging.

JOHN PRIMERANO

As a boy watching the Danny Thomas sitcom, *Make Room*

for Daddy, I especially enjoyed the episodes that wound up on a nightclub floor in Danny's role as an entertainer.

One particular episode was an appearance by Frankie Laine. I recall the ending of the show vividly.

Danny Thomas and Frankie Laine dueted on a "cooking" rendition of "Up Above My Head". Their performance touched the very marrow of my being and I wanted to climb through the face of the tv set to join them.

As great as Danny Thomas was, it was Frankie Laine who added the spark that sent chills through my body. Laine made that number "swing" so effectively that I am quite sure even the *extra's* who were the *patrons* on the nightclub floor felt his powerful delivery and his hand motions caused me to shout, "Yeah!"

John Primerano

Frankie Laine had been a regular in our home as we played his recordings including a favorite "Moonlight Gambler" that painted a picture for me of great singing.

By way of my inclusion in Richard Grudens book *The Italian Crooners Bedside Companion* I was able to have correspondence with Frankie Laine. He had referred to me in the introduction he wrote for the book and was told he liked my composition "Saloon Song."
It's hard to express what that meant to me, that he was aware of me and my work.

So many years after that *Danny Thomas Show* I had the good fortune of becoming acquainted with Frankie Laine which I treasure as one of the highlights of my life and career.

Mr. Laine's last public performance on a PBS Special was simply wonderful. I was able to tell him that and he responded graciously, always the gentleman. I considered it a rare gift to do so, like the man himself.

CHRIS VALENTI - Big Band Broadcaster

Being a Big Band aficionado there are way too many vocalists and talents I truly love and consider being the best. Here is a very short list.

I love Bob Eberly, Dick Haymes, Don Cornell, Perry Como, Billy Eckstine; I could go on writing these names all day. But here is the problem.

There is no vocalist as genuinely multi-dimensional or as categorically diverse as Frankie Laine.

All mentioned above are unique gems and wonderful talents that will continue to carry on our great American musical heritage well into the 22nd century and beyond.

But I must say that Mr. Laine has touched so many more than just the immediate and predictable audiences of the above. I say this for many reasons aside from his amazing musical diversity.

Most importantly was his personal warmth and sincerity he so casually intertwined within his talent and conviction.

This rare talent touched every genre and generation he spoke to. He was from the heart.

This is an *unknowing* talent only God can hand down. Frankie had it… and may not have even known he did. God bless Frankie Laine.

Chris Valenti

PAT BOONE

I went to New York and I sang " I Believe" at the Ted Mack Amateur Hour and *won*. Came back the next week and the next and then eventually won the *Arthur Godfrey Talent Show* contest and I went to Las

Pat Boone

Vegas to perform, following Frankie Laine. So I went the night before and saw him perform and watched him wrap up the audience in the palm of his hand just singing his great hits including "I Believe. " I met him afterwards when I went into his dressing room and he was in his robe and relaxing and told him what a fan and how I'd sung "I Believe." He was very encouraging. He was aware that I had some record success and that I was coming in the next night to open, and he said, "You'll love this place, the people are fine, family kind of people and you'll go over great with it so don't worry. He tried to put me at ease because he sensed that I was a little nervous, especially following him!

Fortunately it wasn't the very same audience and I performed the next night and we had a great engagement. But, I will never forget how warm, supportive and encouraging he was to me, a kid, who was trying to follow - in a way - his footsteps. I even sang "Jezebel." You could imagine what that must've been like for a high school kid singing "Jezebel." But, you know, these were hit songs and Frankie Laine was the hit maker. I'll never forget him.

Doris Day

I was in the seventh grade and it was "That's My Desire." And you could not turn on the radio and not hear that song. And, all of us was just in love with him and then, never knowing that I would be able to work with him and get to know such a lovely man was gold for me. We made a few sides together and one of them, "Sugarbush" went straight to the top of the charts and even sold over one million copies that earned it a Gold Record.

Doris Day

Frankie was a delight to work with. He made it look so easy because he believed in every word he sang and he sang every word with his heart.

GMMY RADIO

GMMY Radio is the enlightening brainchild of Frank E. Dee who hails from New England and has been a saloon singer and has produced comedy and legitimate theater. A writer and weekly newspaper manager most of his career, Frank became a radio host under the tutelage of legendary Bill Marlowe.

Living in California in the 1990s Frank set up the Golden Memories of Yesteryear (GMMY) radio in 2004, broadcasting nostalgic big band sounds of the 30s, 40s, & 50s worldwide with the assistance of a handful of radio hosts who believe his "slice of Heaven." They have all participated in this tribute to Frankie Laine for whom they have dedicated programs and special segments to their formats. Their coverage stretches from California to Pennsylvania, Iowa, Arizona, Boston, Mass., and Italy.

ALAN BROWN - Radio Personality, England

Frankie Laine was a man's singer. Why do I say that, well he had the most macho image of all the singers of that era.

A big guy with a big voice. When he hit the airwaves with "Jezebel" he stamped his authority on singing that type of song, nobody could come anywhere near him. The thing was that his first release "That's My Desire" was completely different. His album "You

Are My Love" with the Frank Comstock orchestra proves he could sing a ballad as good as the rest. It happens to be my favorite album by him.

Frankie Laine was a great vocalist with a huge following whom we will never see the likes of again.

GIULIANO FOURNIER - Radio Host in Italy

In the 50s, I lived in Verona, Italy. At that time there were no discos or clubs for teenagers. The only way to meet the other sex was on Saturday or Sunday afternoon at home and have our private party. In Italy they were called "Festine" (little party).

The music was a simple, bulky turntable with large lighted sides for bottles and other family souvenirs. Someone was always ready to change the 78 rpm records and being very careful not to break them.

The music were songs of the moment, music taken from films such as "Gunfight at OK Corral," "Blowing Wild," and the voice we loved to hear was the booming voice of Frankie Laine.

Frankie Laine was for me an artist living on another planet. If someone had told me that one day I would actually meet the man, I would have laughed.

It was beautiful and haunting to hear the words "Marina Mine" from "Blowing Wild," "Granada," "Mam'selle," "I Believe." "Jezebel," and "High Noon."

Then I started working for Swiss Radio in Lugano, Switzerland with a broadcast called "Broadway, Hollywood, Las Vegas" two hours live every Sunday.

I began in 1973 with the help of a great friend, the great bandleader Stan Kenton. He allowed me an interview and that's how it started. One day I got Frankie Laine's address, and sent him a letter, even knowing how difficult is to receive a reply. Surprisingly, I received a kind letter with his home phone number. I was thrilled. When I called him, the sound of his voice through the telephone gave me a sensation. That's how our relationship started.

Lately, I had to chance to go to Los Angeles, so I flew on to San Diego to meet the man. What a reception. I met an old friend who invited me to dinner with his sweet wife Marcia and later to his home with a stunning view of the San Diego harbor. I saw his record collection. We talked about his performance in Italy at the Festival of San Remo. What a success!

Then he came up with a bottle of Cabernet Sauvignon, from his cellar. On the bottle was carved "Lo Vecchio Vinery." He signed the bottle and told me to drink the good wine. I didn't, even if I want it very badly.

I still treasure that bottle in my home in Italy.

I remember, every time I called him for a short, live interview on the telephone, his voice saying "come stai, paisano ?" made me feel very happy. Frank even called me at home from time to time. One Christmas I even received a crystal vase with flowers. What a friend, what a man, what a human being.

When he passed away on February 6th, 2007 it was though someone of my family had passed on.

LENA AND HARRY SMITH - RADIO HOSTS

Our personal admiration of Frankie's colossal talent began mainly from his early fifties recordings.

We were totally spellbound by the powerful tones and exuberance of songs such as "Jealousy" "High Noon" and "I Believe," songs that could not fail to transport and elevate us to the heavens, and then in complete contrast, with perfect and unmatchable phrasing and with that familiar emotional shudder and heartbreak can deliver a ballad that just melt our hearts in a way that few would dare to try.

We were privileged to see the great man twice here in London, and have cherished memories of a voice of unique style and distinction that has brought us so much joy and enriched our lives.
Thank you Frankie Laine. We miss you!

RON DELLA CHIESA - WGBH BOSTON, WPLM, PLYMOUTH -
Legendary Radio Host

In the late '50s and '60s Frankie Laine was one of America's top male singers. His real name was Paul Lo Vecchio, and like many other Italian-American singers he came from a poor family in Chicago.

I always enjoyed his rich sounding baritone voice at times almost operatic in quality.

One of the first times I heard him was on the radio singing the title song from the movie High Noon." It impressed me so much I went out and bought the record and became a lifelong fan. Whatever he sang, Frankie always poured his heart and soul into every song.
Like his early idol Al Jolson, he could knock out his audiences and always leave them wanting more! He was also a marvelous Jazz singer. My favorite Laine album is Jazz Spectacular, a jam session with Jazz great Buck Clayton that he recorded for Columbia in the late '50s.

He sings standards like "My Old Flame," "Roses of Picardy," "If You Were Mine," and "Stars Fell on Alabama," and proves that when he wanted to be he was one of the best Jazz singer's in the business.

Frankie Laine will forever be heard on my Musicamerica Show.

He was truly one of our all time greats.

DICK AND SHIRLEY FINNELL - RADIO HOSTS

My dad and I saw Frankie Laine perform in either 1951 or 52 at the Stanley Theater in Pittsburgh. Once each month the Stanley would bring in big names for a 7PM show, and he was outstanding. My dad had his barbershop in the basement of our home in Pittsburgh, Pa. in the forties and early fifties. I had a portable record player that he would take downstairs almost every day. He would play records of his favorite singers, mostly Frankie Laine. After he closed the shop on Saturday afternoon, we would walk down to Verneci's Music Store to see if there were any new Laine records.

Dick and Shirley Finnell with Al Martino

My dad passed in 1953 and his greatest gift to me was his love of good music.

Shirley and I were lucky to see Frankie's final appearance on PBS. He sang "That's My Desire". He was 92 years old. The performance impressed us as we have always enjoyed his singing, but this particular show remains in our hearts and minds.

FRANK SINCLAIR - RADIO HOST

Frankie Laine was a man who began with humble origins, born on March 30, 1913, in the city of Chicago.

His love of music started early as a member of the chorus of the Immaculate Conception Elementary School, and as an altar boy at the Church of the Immaculate Conception. Indeed, Frankie truly knew he wanted to become a singer one day, when he cut class at Lane Technical High School, and saw the 1928 Al Jolson classic movie: *The Singing Fool*.

Frankie was known for singing a number of different musical styles, from pop, to jazz, to rhythm and blues, as well as his memorable country-inspired classics. One of the first things Laine did to delve into the world of music was to join the Merry Garden's marathon dance company. There, he honed not only his dancing skills, but in 1932, he earned a world record for marathon dancing of 3501 hours with his partner Ruthie Smith. During his marathon dancing days, he also entertained people during the little breaks the dancers took every hour.

Frankie Laine also had some very interesting early influences, such as Bessie Smith, who had a vastly different sound to what he was accustomed to hearing. Interesting that he found Smith's record: "The Bleeding Hearted Blues" among those in his parents' collection, but he claimed that was his first exposure to jazz and the blues as musical forms. Frankie also picked up ideas of music from Bing Crosby, as well as Billie Holiday, and other black acts. Thus, with his earthy baritone voice, he began to sing in a style altogether different from the crooners of the time. It was more of an energy filled style, which may well in turn have influenced later R & B singers, while distancing himself, stylistically, from the likes of Frank Sinatra.

Things were slowly coming together for Laine, and in 1937, he replaced Perry Como in Freddie Carlone's band until he moved to Los Angeles, where in 1947, Hoagy Carmichael heard Frankie sing his own "Rocking Chair." He went on to record "That's My Desire," which became Frankie's first smash hit, launching him on to stardom. In 1953, he achieved a tremendous hit with "I Believe," a song which remained number one in the United Kingdom for an unprecedented 18 weeks, something even the Beatles could not best!

With more than 100 Million records sold, Frankie Laine was a legend of his time, and on his 80th birthday, the United States Congress declared him a National Treasure. In 2005, he appeared in the PBS special: "My Music", where he sang the song that started it all for him, and making him come full circle: "That's My Desire." Although rock historian types have rarely acknowledged Laine's influence on Rock and Roll music, his early singing of "Race Music" helped open the door for other white singers who decided to sing in the black style, and which in turn, helped to open up the doors of opportunity for a myriad of black artists that followed.

Sadly, the world lost a tremendous man and talent, Frankie Laine, when he died of heart failure on February 6, 2007, but not before he cemented his place in the pantheon of the truly great American singing stars.

OLD SHOES
AND
OLD TRUMPETS

One day, back in 1998, Frankie Laine made a plea over the radio asking for donations of shoes for the homeless. He was eighty-four at the time and had recently released the single recording "This Dream's On Me."

Well, his plea was heard by many including Victor Pinzon, an official with the Salvation Army who got in touch with Frankie, and together they formed a union they called The Old Shoe Program. It was very successful campaign and was extended nationally through the auspices of the Salvation Army.

"I got started in 1991 when I was watching a newscast and they showed a cop rousting a guy off a park bench. As the guy ran off, I noticed the soles of his shoes were flapping and thought of my own days back In New York when I wasn't far from that condition myself." He immediately donated 20 pair of his own shoes.

This was typical of Frankie's approach to life. He often entertained seniors at various functions, and at nursing homes and hospitals, but at a much lower pace. He felt that many people of his generation were lonely and forgotten and needed extra medical care and special needs - like shoes.

His other charity, the after-school program to provide musical instruments for disadvantaged children was just as successful as his shoes appeal, when his plea over the radio, once again, brought donations of instruments to the Salvation Army offices to enhance its children's music programs.

The voice of a great celebrity like Frankie Laine can move mountains when the need is there. And so he fulfilled his promises in that way.

Frank was also affiliated with the Meals on Wheels program in his area.

Among his charities were a series of local benefit concerts that provided assistance with homeless shelters, and work with St. Vincent de Paul Village. He was an emeritus member of the Board of Directors of Mercy Hospital Foundation.

with Secretary of Navy
Benevolent Fund

with Secretary of Damon
Runyon Cancer Fund

THE FRANKIE LAINE INTERNATIONAL APPRECIATION SOCIETY

A MESSAGE FROM TONY COOPER

There has always been a Frankie Laine Society of some sort in the UK since 1952. However FLIAS in its present form was charted in 1972 when Frankie returned to Europe in 1974 after a 17 year gap. The society really took off at this point.

So, instead of it being run by a few members, in 1976 we had to expand.

We were now able to produce albums for sale to members which consisted of unissued and extremely rare material taken from radio, TV and live performances.

We have always searched out Laine material from all over the world and now have one of the largest archives of any artist, which we try to make available for members to purchase.

We have issued over 25 videos/DVD/s with concerts, TV appearances et al from 1950 right up to his parting in 2007 and continue to find material thought lost since the 1940s.

During Frankie's tours we arranged prefferential seating for members and the opportunity to meet and chat with Frankie after those concerts. We also hold two conventions a year, one in the north and one in the south of England. Members also travel frequently abroad to visit with fans from other countries.

Rosie Carden and I are still running the society with Rosie attending to publishing the magazine and I arranging DVD/CD releases for the members and advising record companies as to what material should be issued for maximum sales.

One benefit of becoming a Frankie Laine fan and also a member of FLIAS is the number of friends you can make who live all over the world.

I have had the pleasure of such friendships from places like Australia, South Africa, many Far East countries and the whole of Europe. A number of these wonderful friends have visited my wife Pam and I at our home and have developed into lifelong friends. There is Heinz Grundel (Munich, Germany), Joachim Senkler (Cuxhaven), both great German Frankie Laine fans, Richard LeBlond, who dubs the voice of Harrison Ford and others when their films are shown in France, and Piet Cramer, a longtime friend from Holland. All these and many, many others, all dedicated fans of the great Frankie Laine have met and through a common bond, become friends of Frankie Laine and of one another.

Come join us.

Tony Cooper 18 Napier Crescent, Seamer, Scarborough, North Yorkshire YO12 4AY

LAINE LINES No.134   August 2007

FLIAS COMMITTEE OFFICERS:
Chairman: Rosemary Carden
Silsden Cottage, London Road,
Chalfont St. Giles, Buckinghamshire, HP8 4ND
       (Office Hours) Telephone:01494 872056
Treasurer / Membership Secretary: Tony Cooper
18 Napier Crescent, Seamer, Scarborough,
    North Yorkshire. YO12 4HY   Telephone: 01723 863022
Hon. Secretary: Annette Walker
8 Barley Close, Henley-in-Arden, Warwickshire B95 5HU
       Telephone: 01564 792837

Paul Durham
Rouseau Ouest,
33580 Cours de Monsegur
FRANCE
email at: marjori.durham@orange.fr
Telephone: 0033 553 64 49 10

GENERAL COMMITTEE MEMBERS:
Alec Furzer - Milton Keynes   Telephone: 01908 641242
Alan Inns - Chesterfield   Telephone: 01246   31499
Eddie Torr - Rotherham   Telephone: 01709 530328
Glyn Walker
8 Barley Close, Henley-in-Arden,   Warwickshire B95 5HU
       Telephone: 01564 792837
PROJECT LEADERS (co-opted volunteers)
Discography: Bert Boorman

Films: Ron Carden Silsden Cottage, London Road,
Chalfont St. Giles, Buckinghamshire, HP8 4ND
       (Office Hours) Telephone:01494 872056

Specials: Ken Prewitt
FRANKIE LAINE SOCIETY OF AMERICA
President:Victoria Lockridge,
PO Box 7996, North Torrance Station,
Torrance Ca. 90504, U.S.A

Slipped Disk
by Marvin

After more than four years of writing this column I guess it's all right to repeat once in a while. And when the artist is Frankie Laine, truly one of our 'living legends', and he's about to celebrate his 75th birthday - well, it's time to again praise this charming man.

On March 30th, 1988, friends and fans of Mr. Laine will be meeting in San Diego to usher in a new year for "Mr. Rhythm". Seventy devoted fans from England and the Netherlands will be flying over to attend this function. Frankie and Nan will be there, of course.

There are many fine Frankie Laine albums to satisfy your taste. There's the "Greatest Hits" album on Columbia (Col. 9636) and "Torchin'" on Columbia is also still available. The early Mercury days are captured on many repackaged LP's. It won't be difficult to find Frankie Laine recordings of "Mule Train", "Satan Wore A Satin Gown", or "That's My Desire."

Many of the old favorites have been revived for some recent concerts. Last August, for example, at Eisenhower Park (NY) there were an estimated 30,000 fans. During the evening they were treated to revivals of "Black and Blue", "Baby, Baby all the Time", and "Music, Maestro, Please". What a sensational night that must have been.

FRANKIE LAINE

A recent album by Frankie Laine places him in a slightly different field. In **"A Country Laine"** (Sutra Playback Record PLL 12004), Mr. Laines brings his skill and style to such favorites as "Jambalaya", "Old Dogs, Children and Watermelon Wine", "Green, Green Grass of Home", "Another Somebody Done Somebody Wrong Song", and others.

This fine album was produced by Jack Gale, Jim Pierce and Ken Hart. Frankie Laine was the Executive Producer. The recordings were made at Swanee Recording, Mt. Juliet, Tenn.

It's good - it's recent - and, most of all, it's Frankie Laine.

We're a bit early for this but:

HAPPY 75th BIRTHDAY FRANKIE LAINE!

THE FRANKIE LAINE TEAM

L-R: Jimmy Marino, Barbara Marino, Mary Jo-Coombs, Dorothy Hollman, Benny Hollman

The author wishes to express his appreciation to the Frankie Laine Team comprised of Jimmy Marino (Producer/Business Manager), Barbara Marino (Office/Marketing), Mary-Jo Coombs (Frankie's Personal Assistant), Dorothy Hollman (Event Assistant), and Benny Hollman (Musical Arranger/Conductor), who have had the privilege of working personally with Frankie Laine over many years and who have dedicated themselves to "Keeping Frankie Laine's Music Alive!"

Without their sincere efforts and purpose this book may not have been written. They have provided much of the material to form this fitting tribute. Their enthusiasm and love for Frankie Laine and his music is humble, clear, and beautiful.

MARCIA AND FRANKIE LAINE - 1999

The day I walked into his home I felt so comfortable. I had heard from everybody that he was a nice, warm individual. Frankie had no phony bones in his body and he loved everyone. Everyone. I've been twice blessed because I had a wonderful husband for thirty-two years, and the time I had with Frank was just too short but wonderful. I wish he was still here. Frank's oldest daughter Pamela lives in Sherman Oaks in the San Fernando Valley. His youngest, Jan, lives with her physician husband in retirement.

Marcia

EULOGY

Rosemary Carden's Eulogy

Frank taught us much about life - nobody owes you anything, you have to get out and earn it. When the going gets tough, don't let it get you down, get on with it. He never forgot his hard times and those who helped him along the way. The following good years were "pay back " time as far as he was concerned and pay back he certainly did in many ways by helping those less fortunate than himself.

He taught us to never give up on ourselves -there were occasions when he almost gave up but that inborn instinct to meet whatever challenge life threw at him came to the fore. It was not in his character to give in, quiet determination to overcome was the order of the day. Hilaire Belloc wrote: "It is the best of all trades to make songs, and the second best to sing them." Frank fulfilled both criteria, such was his talent.

He may be leaving us for a while physically, but he will never be far away and we will be together again - his spirit lives on in us. His music, friendship and love surrounds us. His legacy is more precious than worldly good; each of us has special memories - a host of them funny, some almost serious! All of them are a precious gift form him. Percy Bysche Shelley wrote "music, when soft voices die, vibrates in the memory."

This world has been a better place for having Frankie Laine, alias F.P. LoVecchio, in it and we are so very privileged to have had him with us for such a long time.

Frank, you have been an inspiration to millions of people around the troubled world-music makes the world go round as the saying goes, and you certainly proved that.

William Shakespeare wrote: "We are such stuff as dreams are made on, and our little life is rounded with a sleep." Sleep well dearest friend. Arrivederci. Te amo.

(Read by Jimmy Marino at the Memorial Service.)

TRIBUTE
"I AM A SINGER."

At this point in the proceedings, we would like to leave you with the lyrics of a song, which embodies the musical life of Frankie Laine. It is entitled, 'I Am A Singer' and was originally recorded by Jack Jones in 1987. (Jack Jones, incidentally, was a protégé of Frankie Laine's.) For those who attended Frankie's 85th birthday celebration, or who were lucky enough to see Frankie at his second engagement at The Orleans in Las Vegas, he explained in his introduction to the song, how well it expressed his feelings about being on stage and singing. It is a song that truly hit an emotional chord with Frankie, and one that he had intended to record. As always, the lyrics, though simple, gained tremendous depth when he sang them. As you read these lyrics, know that he was speaking to each and every person who ever saw him perform on a stage:

I AM A SINGER
(G. Kenny / D. Shephard)

I am a Singer.
I work at night.
I stand in front of you,
And hold my notes up to the light.
I tune up all my secrets,
And hang them on my voice,
I have no other talent,
I have no other choice,
I am a Singer.

I do the ballads.
I do the blues.
You know, no matter what,
I've got a song for you to use.
I step inside my feelings,
And spread my story out,
And when the chorus calls me,
It proves without a doubt,
I am a Singer.

I remember every melody
That ever danced my way,
From last night's solo concert
To my part in the high school play.
I remember every songbook
That I lived through page by page,
And how I came to love you
Once you let me on the stage . . .

I'm a Singer.
I sing your songs.
I bring the words to life,
And keep the beat where it belongs.
I work for your attention,
And wait for your applause,
You have me by my music,
And I need your love because

I am a Singer,
I am a Singer,
I am a Singer.

Gratefully,
Frankie Laine

BIBLIOGRAPHY

Dana, Robert W. *Craig's Big Band & Big Names.com*

Dunning, John. *On The Air -The Encyclopedia of Old-Time Radio* vg New York, N.Y: Oxford University Press. 1998

George, Don *Sweet Man-the Real Duke Ellington*. New York, New York: G.P. Putnam's Sons. 1981

Grudens, Richard. *The Best Damn Trumpet Player*, Stonybrook, New York 11790. Celebrity Profiles Publishing Company. 1997

Grudens, Richard. *Stardust-The Bible of the Big Bands.* Stonyrook, New York 11790
2007

James, Gary. Gary James Interview - www.famousinterview.com

Laine, Frankie & Joseph Laredo., *That Lucky Old Son* Ventura, California: Path-finder Publishing Company. 1993

Lerner, Al. *Vamp 'Til Ready* Albany, GA: Bear Manor Media, 2007

Murrells, Joseph. *Million Selling Records - An Illustrated Directory*. New York, NY: Arco Publishing, Inc. 1984

O'Day, Anita, George Eells, *High Times Hard Times*. New York, N.Y.: C.P. Put-nam's Sons. 1981

Pleasants, Henry. *The Great American Popular Singers.* New York, N.Y.: Simon and Schuster. 1974

Shaw, Arnold. 52nd Street, The Street of Jazz. New York, N.Y., DeCapo Press. 1971

Whiteside, Jonny, *Cry: The Johnnie Ray Story*, New York, New York: Barricade Books, Inc. 1994

THE SINGLES

Label/Record#/Title		Release Date
Gold Seal		
GS7262	In The Wee Small Hours/That's Liberty	1944
Atlas		
FL127	Melancholy Madeline/Maureen	1945
FL137	Someday Sweetheart/Baby, Baby All The Time	1945
FL141	I'm Confessin'/Heartaches	1945
FL142	Coquette/It Ain't Gonna Be Like That	1945
FL147	S'posin'/You've Changed	1945
FL148	Oh! Lady Be Good/You Can Depend On Me	1945
FL156	Moonlight in Vermont/Roses of Picardy	1945
Mercury		
3016	I May Be Wrong/(Another Artist)	1946
5003	September in the Rain/Ain't That Just Like A Woman	1946
5007 (GR)	That's My Desire/By The River Saint Marie	1946
5015	Texas & Pacific/(Another Artist)	1947
5018	Sunday Kind Of Love/Who Cares What People Say?	1947
5028	I May Be Wrong/Stay As Sweet As You Are	1947
1027 (GR)	On The Sunny Side Of The Street/Blue Turning Grey Over You	1947

1028	West End Blues/I Can't Believe You're In Love With Me	1947
1178	I'm In The Mood For Love/Cherie, I Love You	1947
1180	Rockin' Chair/Till We Meet Again	1947
5048	Mam'selle/All Of Me	1947
5059	Kiss Me Again/By The Light Of The Stars	1947
5064(GR)	Two Loves Have I/Put Yourself in My Place	1947
5091(GR)	Shine/We'll Be Together Again	1948
5096	But Beautiful/I've Only Myself to Blame	1948
5105	I'm Looking Over A Four Leaf Clover/Monday Again	1948
5114	That Ain't Right/May I Never Love Again	1948
5130	Put 'em In A Box/Baby, Don't Be Mad At Me	1948
5158	Ah, But It Happens/Hold Me	1948
5174	Singing The Blues/Thanks For You	1948
5177	You're All I Want For Christmas/Tara Talara Tala	1948
5227	Rosetta/It Only Happens Once	1949
5243	Wish You Were Jealous Of Me/Don't Have To Tell Nobody	1949
5275	September In The Rain/Sweet Talk	1949
5293	Georgia On My Mind/You're Just the Kind	1949
5301	Nevertheless/Bebop Spoken Here	1949
5311	Now That I Need You/My Own, My Only, My All	1949
5316(GR)	That Lucky Old Sun/I Get Sentimental Over Nothing	1949
5332	Waiting At The End of the Road/Don't Do Something To Somebody Else	1949
5345(GR)	Mule Train/Carry Me Back to Old Virginny	1949
5355	God Bless the Child/Don't Cry Little Children	1950
5358	Satan Wears A Satin Gown/Baby Just For Me	1950
5363(GR)	Cry of the Wild Goose/Black Lace	1950
5390(GR)	Swamp Girl/Give Me A Kiss For Tomorrow	1950
5421	Stars & Stripes Forever/Thanks For Your Kisses	1950
5442	If I Were You Baby/I Love You For That (with Patti Page)	1950
5495	Nevertheless/I Was Dancing With Someone	1950
5500	Sleepy Ol' River/If I Were A Bell	1950
5544	I'm Gonna Live Till I Die/A Man Gets Awfully Lonesome	1950
5553	Merry Christmas Everywhere/What Am I Gonna Do This Christmas?	1950

5580	May The Good Lord Bless and Keep You/Dear Dear, Dear	1951
5581	Metro Polka/The Jalopy Song	1951
5656	Heart Of My Heart/You Left Me Out In The Rain	1951
5685	Isle Of Capri/The Day Isn't Long Enough	1951
5733	Get Happy/I Would Do Most Anything For You	1951
5768	Baby I Need You/South of the Border	1951
70099	Ain't Misbehavin'/That's How Rhythm Was Born	1951

Columbia

39367(2 GRs)	Jezebel/Rose, Rose I Love You	1951
39388	Pretty-Eyed Baby/That's The One For Me (with Jo Stafford)	1951
39466	In The Cool, Cool, Cool, of the Evening/That's Good! That's Bad! (with Jo Stafford)	1952
39693	Sugarbush/How Lovely Cooks the Meat (with Doris Day)	1952
39716	Snow In Lover's Lane/That's How It Goes	1952
39770 (GR)	High Noon/Rock of Giblralter	1952
39798	Rainbow Around My Shoulder/She's Funny That Way	1952
39862	The Mermaid/The Ruby and the Pearl	1952
39867	Settin' the Woods on Fire/Piece-A-Puddin (with Jo Stafford)	1952
39893	Chow Willy/Christmas Roses (with Jo Stafford)	1952
39903	I'm Just A Poor Bachelor/Tonight You Belong To Me	1952
39938 (2GRs)	I Believe/Your Cheatin' Heart	1953
39945	Tell Me A Story/Little Boy and the Old Man (with Jimmy Boyd)	1953
39979	Ramblin' Man/I Let Her Go	1953
40022	Where the Winds Blow/Te Amo	1953
40036	Poor Little Piggy Bank/Let's Go Fishin' (with Jimmy Boyd)	1953
40079	Answer Me O Lord/Blowing Wild	1953
40116	Way Down Yonder In New Orleans/Floating Down to Cotton Town (with Jo Stafford)	1952
40136	Granada/I'd Give My Life	1954
40178 (GR)	Kid's Last Fight/Long Distance Love	1954
40198	Goin' Like Wildfire/Rollin' Down the Line (with Jo Stafford)	1954
40235	Someday/There Must Be A Reason	1954

40295	Rain Rain, Rain/Your Heart, My Heart (with The Four Lads)	1954
40378	Old Shoes/In the Beginning'	1955
40401	High Society/Back Where I Belong (with Jo Stafford)	1955
40413	Keepin' Out Of Mischief/I Can't Give You Anything But Love	1955
40433	Bubbles/Tarrier Song	1955
40457(GR)	Cool Water/Strange Lady in Town	1955
40526	Hummingbird/My Little One	1955
40539	Mona Lisa/Laura	1955
40558	Hawkeye/Your Love	1955
40583(GR)	A Woman In Love/Walking The Night Away	1955
40600	Ain't It A Pity and a Shame/I Heard the Angels Singing (with The Four Lads)	1955
40650	Little Child/Let's Go Fishin'	1955
50006	Jezebel/Jealousy	1955
50038	High Noon/I Believe	1955
40663	Hell Hath No Fury/The Most Happy Fella	1956
40669	Moby Dick/A Capital Ship	1956
40693	Don't Cry/Ticky Ticky Tick	1956
J4-275	Robin Hood/Champion The Wonder Horse	1956
40720	Make Me A Child Again/The Thief	1956
40741	On the Road To Mandalay/Only If We Love	1956
40780(GR)	Moonlight Gambler/Lotus Land	1956
40856	Love Is a Golden Ring/There's Not A Moment To Spare	1957
40916	Gunfight At the O.K. Corral/Without Him	1957
40962	The 3:10 To Yuma/You Know How It Is	1957
40976	Good Evening Friends/Up Above My Head (with Johnny Ray)	1957
41036	The Greater Sin/East is East	1957

Mercury

30017	That Lucky Old Sun/Shine	1957
30018	Mule Train/Cry of the Wild Goose	1957
30019	That's My Desire/By the River Saint Marie	1957

Columbia

41106	Annabel Lee/All of These and More	1958
41139	My Gal and a Prayer/The Lonesome Road	1958
41163	Lovin' Up A Storm/A Kiss Can Change the World	1958
41187	Choombala Bay/I Have To Cry	1958
41230(GR)	Rawhide/Magnificent Obsession	1958

41283	Midnight On A Rainy Monday/When I Speak Your Name	1958
41331	That's My Desire/In My Wildest Dreams	1958
41376	Journey's Ended/My Little Love	1959
41430	El Diablo/Valley of a Hundred Hills	1959
41486	Rocks and Gravel/Rockin' Mother	1959
41613	St. James Infirmary/Et Voila	1960
41700	Seven Women/Doesn't She Roll	1960
41787	Here She Comes Now/Kisses That Shake The World	1961
41974	Gunslinger/Wanted Man	1961
42233	Miss Satan/Ride Through The Night	1961
3-33009	Your Cheating Heart/Jezebel	1961
42383	Wedded Man/We'll Be Together Again	1962
42767	Don't Make My Baby Blue/The Moment of Truth	1963

Mercury

30056	Georgia On My Mind/September in the Rain	1963
30062	All of Me/When You're Smiling	1963

Columbia

42884	Take Her She's Mine/I'm Gonna Be Strong	1964
42966	Up Among The Stars/Lonely Days of Winter	1964

Capitol

5299	Halfway/Go On with Your Dancing	1964
5472	House of Laughter/A Girl	1964
5525	Seven Days of Love/Heartaches Can Be Fun	1965
5569	The Meaning of It All/Pray and He Will Answer You	1966
5658	Johnny Willow/What Do You Know?	1966

ABC

10891	I'll Take Care of Your Cares/Every Street's A Boulevard	1967
10924(GR)	Making Memories/The Moment of Truth	1967
10946	You Wanted Someone To Play With/The Real True Meaning of Love	1967
10967	Laura/Sometimes I Just Can't Stand You	1967
10983	You, No One But You/Somewhere There's Someone	1967
11032	To Each His Own/I'm Happy to Hear You're Sorry	1968
11057	I Found You/I Don't Want To Set the World on Fire	1968
11097	Take Me Back/Forsaking All Others	1968
11129	Please Forgive Me/Pretty Little Princess	1968

11174(GR)	Lord, You Gave Me A Mountain/The Secret of Happiness	1969
11224	Dammit Isn't God's Last Name/Fresh Out of Tears	1969
11234	Allegra/If I Didn't Believe In You	1970
11231	I'll Take Care of Your Cares/Making Memories	1970

Amos

AJB138	I Believe/On the Sunny Side of the Street	1970
AJB153	Put Your Hand in the Hand/Going To Newport	1971
AJB161	Don't Blame the Child/My God and I	1971

Score

| SC5059 | Can You Hear Me Lord?/Going To Newport | 1972 |

Sunflower

| SNF125 | My Own True Love/Time To Ride | 1973 |

Warner Brothers

| WB7774 | Blazing Saddles/(Another Artist) | 1974 |

Mainstream

| MRL5579 | Talk To Me 'Bout the Hard Times (Parts I & II) | 1976 |

CBS

| TB16306 | If I Never Sing Another Song/We'll Be Together Again | 1981 |

Score

| FLS 201 | Take Me Back to L.A./We'll Be Together Again | 1984 |

Riclew

| RL000A | Strike Up the Band for San Diego/(Another Artist) | 1985 |

Score

| FLS 202 | San Diego, Lovely Lady By the Sea/(Another Artist) | 1985 |
| FLS 203 | Merry Christmas Without You/Old New Orleans | 1986 |

Playback

| PL1106 | Jambalaya/The Green, Green Grass of Home | 1986 |
| PL1107 | She Never Could Dance/I Believe in You | 1986 |

THE ALBUMS AND EPs

Mercury

MG25007	Frankie Laine Sings	1947
MG25026	Frankie Laine	1949
MG25025	Songs From the Heart	1949
MG25026	Frankie Laine	1949
MG25027	Frankie Laine	1949

Columbia

| CL2548 | One For My Baby (6 songs) | 1951 |
| CL6200 | One For My Baby (8 songs) | 1951 |

Mercury

MG25097	Mr. Rhythm	1952
MG25098	Song Favorites by Frankie Laine	1952
MG25124	Music Maestro Please	1952

Columbia

CL 6268	Musical Portrait of New Orleans (10 inch) (with Jo Stafford)	1953
CL578	Musical Portrait of New Orleans (12 inch) (with Jo Stafford)	1954
CL6278	Mr. Rhythm	1954
CL2504	Lover Laine	1955
CL625	Command Performance	1955
CL808	Jazz Spectacular (Re-issued in 1977 as JCL808)	1955
CL861	Frankie Laine and the Four Lads	1956

Mercury

MG20069	Songs by Frankie Laine	1956
MG20080	That's My Desire	1956
MG20083	Songs For People Together	1956
MG20085	Concert Date	1956
MG20105	With All My Heart	1956

Allegro

4132	Frankie Sings	1956

Galaxy

4821	Frankie Sings	1956

Columbia

CL975	Rockin'	1957
CL11156	Foreign Affair (with Michel Legrand)	1958
Cl1176/CS8024	Torchin'	1958

Rondolette

A-21	Frankie Laine Sings	1958

Columbia

CL1231/CS8636 Frankie Laine's Greatest Hits	1958
CL1277/CS8087 Reunion in Rhythm (with Michel Legrand, reissued in 1977 as ACS8087)	1959
CL1317/CS8119 You Are My Love	1959

Rondo

R2015/RS2015 Frankie Laine Sings/Andre Previn Plays	1959

Mercury-Wing

MW12110/SAW16110 Sings His All Time Favorites	1966
MW12202/SRW16202 That's My Desire	1960

Columbia

CL1393/CS8188 Balladeer	1960

CL1615/CS8415 Hell Bent For Leather   1961
CS8496   Deuces Wild   1962
CL1829/CS8629 Call of the Wild   1962
Mercury
MG20578/SR60587 Frankie Laine's Golden Hits   1962
Columbia
CL1962/CS8762 Wanderlust   1963
Harmony
HL7329/HS11129 Roving Gambler   1964
Capitol
T2277/ST2277 I Believe   1965
Mercury-Wing
MR12158/SRW16158 Singing the Blues   1966
SRW16349   Frankie Laine's Greatest Hits   1967
ABC
ABC604/ABCS604 I'll Take Care of Your Cares   1967
Harmony
HL7425/HS11225 Frankie Laine Memories   1968
HL7382/HS11182 That's My Desire   1968
ABC
ABC608/ABCS608 I Wanted Someone To Love   1968
ABC628/ABCS628 To Each His Own   1968
ABCS657   Take Me Back to Laine Country   1968
Tower
T5092/TS5092 Memory Laine   1968
ABC
ABCS682   You Gave Me A Mountain   1969
Harmony
HS11345   I'm Gonna Live Till I Die   1969
Mercury-Wing
PKW2-111 Frankie Laine, The Great Years   1969
Amos
AAS-7009 Frankie Laine's Greatest Hits   1970
AAS-7013 A Brand New Day   1971
ABC
ABCX790-2 20 Incredible Performances   1975
Springboard
SP-4009   Frankie Laine's Greatest Hits   1975
SPX-6011   Frankie Laine Sings His Very Best   1976
ABC
AC-30001   The ABC Collection   1976

Pickwick

SPC-3151	Heartaches Can Be Fun	1977
SPC-3526	That Lucky Old Sun	1978
SPC-3601	You Gave Me A Mountain	1979

Koala

AW14133	Frankie Laine Sings	1979

CBS-Encore

P14391	Too Marvelous For Words	1979

51 West

QR16047	Pick of Frankie Laine	1979

Exact

Ex-242	Frankie Laine's Best	1981

CBS

P-15166	Now and Then	1981

Hindsight

HSR198	The Uncollected Frankie Laine-1947	1984
HSR216	The Uncollected, Volume 2	1985

Score

FLP 101	So Ultra Rare	1984
FLP 102	Frankie Laine's Place In Time	1985

Jubilate

J1506	Frankie's Gold	1985

Playback

PP1 12004	A Country Laine	1986

Score

FLC-2002	New Directions	1988

Score

FLC-2005	Riders in the Sky	1991

SELECTED COMPACT DISCS:

Telarc

CD-80141	Round-Up, with Eric Kunzel and the Cincinnati Pops Orchestra	1987

Columbia

CK 45029	Frankie Laine: 16 Most Requested Songs	1989

Bear Family

BCD 15480	Frankie Laine — On the Trail	1990

Polygram

314 510 435-2	The Frankie Laine Collection — The Mercury Years	1991

Score

FLCD 0691	Frankie Laine and Friends (A Collection of Duets)	1991

BRITAIN:
Polydor
2383-457 20 Memories in Gold 1977
2383-488 Life is Beautiful 1978
Bulldog
BDL 1035 All Of Me (early period Laine compilation) 1984
World RecordClub
SM 531-6 The Frankie Laine Songbook (6 album set) 1979
Castle
CD CST 43 Frankie Laine — The Country Store Collection
(compact disc) 1989
Harmony
HARCD 102 Frankie Laine — Portrait of a Song Stylist
(compact disc) 1989
Prestige
PRCDSP300 Somethin' Old, Somethin' New (compact disc) 1992

HOLLAND:
Arcade
ADEH 91 The World of Frankie Laine 1982

Richard Grudens was initially influenced by Pulitzer Prize dramatist Robert Anderson; New York Herald Tribune columnist Will Cuppy; and detective/mystery novelist Dashiell Hammett, all whom he knew in his early years. Grudens worked his way up from studio page in NBC's studios in New York to news writer for radio news programs, the Bob and Ray Show and the Today Show.

Feature writing for Long Island PM Magazine (1980-86) led to his first book, The Best Damn Trumpet Player - Memories of the Big Band Era. He has written over 100 magazine articles on diverse subjects from interviews with legendary cowboy Gene Autry in Wild West Magazine in 1995 to a treatise on the Beach Boys in the California Highway Patrol Magazine, and countless articles on Bing Crosby, Bob Hope, including a major Hope cover article covering Hope's famous wartime USO tours published in World War II Magazine. He has written extensively about Henry Ford, VE Day, Motorcycle Helmet Safety, DNA History, among other subjects.

His other books include The Song Stars-1997, The Music Men-1998, Jukebox Saturday Night - 1999, Snootie Little Cutie - The Connie Haines Story- 2000, Jerry Vale - A Singer's Life-2001, The Spirit of Bob Hope-2002, Bing Crosby-Crooner of the Çentury - 2003 (which won the Benjamin Franklin Award for Biography-Publishers Marketing Association),and Chattanooga Choo Choo - The Life and Times of the World Famous Glenn Miller Orchestra-2004, The Italian Crooners Bedside Companion in 2005 and When Jolson was King in 2006, Star*Dust - The Bible of the Big Bands in 2008 and now Mr. Rhythm - A Tribute to Frankie Laine.

Commenting about the book Jukebox Saturday Night in 1999, Kathryn (Mrs. Bing) Crosby wrote: "Richard Grudens is the musical historian of our time. Without him, the magic would be lost forever. We all owe him a debt that we can never repay."

Richard Grudens, and his wife Madeline, reside in St. James, New York.

ACKNOWLEDGEMENTS

When a book is born, the many individuals, friends and compatriots, who participated in its formation, must be acknowledged for their contributions, however great or small, as no one person can fully create a book alone.

Madeline and I gratefully thank all of you who have contributed to this extraordinary, dignified tribute to the late, great Frankie Laine. To Jimmy and Barbara Marino, Mary-Jo Coombs and Dorothy and Benny Hollman - The Frankie Laine Team - for initiating this tribute and who enlisted Madeline and I and entrusted us to provide the words and the works.

Special thanks to America's great film star and film director, Clint Eastwood for his kind words and assistance.

To the two societies who have honored Frankie Laine over many years; the Frankie Laine Society of America and the Frankie Laine International Society.

To GMMY Radio host Frank E. Dee for his input and enthusiasm for this project.

Perennial assistants have always been Kathryn Crosby, jazz writers John Tumpak and Jack Lebo, broadcaster DJ, Al Monroe, Swiss Radio Broadcaster Max Wirz, general advisors Bob Incagliato and Jerry Castleman, big band leader and arranger Ben Grisafi, premier DJ Jack Ellsworth, and all-around assistant Robert Grudens.

A special thanks to Deana Lou, Executive Assistant, Malpaso Productions at Warner Bros., for her assistance as liaison with Clint Eastwood.

Extra special thanks to Marcia Laine for her invaluable help.

A note of eternal gratitude and tribute to friends I miss - record collector and historian Joe Pardee; eminent photographer C. Camille Smith; photographer Gus Young.

Finally, goodbye to my mentor and friend Frankie Laine, and as he always said: "May God Bless."

We are grateful to:

Madeline Grudens

Robert Grudens

Ben Grisafi

Bob Incagliato

Jack Ellsworth

Max Wirz

Jerry Castleman

Al Monroe

Jack Lebo

Camille Smith

Kathryn Crosby

Frank E. Dee

Additional Titles by Richard Grudens
www.RichardGrudens.com
Explore the Golden Age of Music when the Big Bands and their vocalists reigned on the radio and all the great stages of America.

Chattanooga Choo Choo - The Life and Times of the World Famous Glenn Miller Orchestra

Commemorating the 100th Anniversary of Glenn Miller's life and the 60th Anniversary of his disappearance over the English Channel in late 1944, we present the tribute book Glenn Miller fans all over the world have been waiting for.

Bing Crosby - Crooner of the Century

Here is the quintessential Bing Crosby tribute, documenting the story of Crosby's colorful life, family, recordings, radio and television shows, and films; the amazing success story of a wondrous career that pioneered popular music spanning generations and inspiring countless followers.

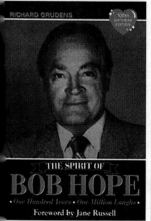

The Spirit of Bob Hope:

Tracing Bob's charmed life from his early days in Cleveland to his worldwide fame earned in vaudeville, radio, television and films and his famous wartime travels for the USO unselfishly entertaining our troops. The best Bob Hope book with testimonials from his friends and a foreword by Jane Russell.

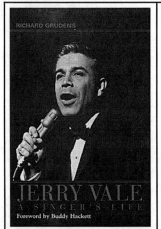

Jerry Vale - A Singer's Life

The wondrous story of Jerry's life as a kid from teeming Bronx streets of the 1940s to his legendary appearances in the great theatrical venues of America and his three triumphant Carnegie Hall concerts, with appearances at New York's Copacabana, whose magnificent voice has beautifully interpreted the 20th Century's most beautiful love songs

Snootie Little Cutie - The Connie Haines Story

The story of big band singer, Connie Haines, who sang shoulder to shoulder with Frank Sinatra in the bands of Harry James and Tommy Dorsey, and for years on the Abbott & Costello radio show, and who is still singing today.

Jukebox Saturday Night

The final book in the series; interviews with Artie Shaw, Les Brown and Doris Day, Red Norvo, Les Paul, Carmel Quinn, stories about Glenn Miller and the Dorsey Brothers, songwriters Ervin Drake ("I Believe," "It was a Very Good Year,") and Jack Lawrence ("Linda," "Tenderly,") and a special about all the European bands past and present.

Sally Bennett's Magic Moments

This book is filled with extraordinary events in the life of Sally Bennett who established the Big Band Hall of Fame and Museum in West Palm Beach, Florida. Sally is a composer, musician, playwright, model, actress, poet, radio and TV personality and the author of the book *Sugar and Spice.*

The Music Men

A Companion to "The Song Stars," about the great men singers with foreword by Bob Hope; interviews with Tony Martin, Don Cornell, Julius LaRosa, Jerry Vale, Joe Williams, Johnny Mathis, Al Martino, Guy Mitchell, Tex Beneke and others.

The Song Stars

A neat book about all the girl singers of the Big Band Era and beyond: Doris Day, Helen Forrest, Kitty Kallen, Rosemary Clooney, Jo Stafford, Connie Haines, Teresa Brewer, Patti Page and Helen O'Connell and many more.

The Best Damn Trumpet Player

Memories of the Big Band Era, interviews with Benny Goodman, Harry James, Woody Herman, Tony Bennett, Buddy Rich, Sarah Vaughan, Lionel Hampton, Frankie Laine, Patty Andrews and others.

Star*Dust - The Bible of the Big Bands

A discussion of forty of our twentieth century's big bands, including Glenn Miller, Benny Goodman, Artie Shaw, Les Brown, Stan Kenton, Tommy Dorsey, Jimmy Dorsey, Duke Ellington, Woody Herman, Buddy Rich, Harry James, Van Alexander, Jack Teagarden, Ben Grisafi, Lionel Hampton, many of its most famous musicians, thirty-eight of its greatest vocalists, including a centerpiece on Frank Sinatra and Bing Crosby, their associates and arrangers, together with their predecessors, followers, and European counterparts.

Mr. Rhythm - A Tribute to Frankie Laine - Foreword by Clint Eastwood

This book celebrates the life and times and sights and sounds of Frankie Laine: the trials, the rejections, the heartbreak, the hard work, and eventual victory, punctuated by all the complexities that make up the ubiquitous profession called show business. The foreword is written by one of America's greatest film stars, five time Academy Award winning actor and director, Clint Eastwood, an admirer and true friend of Frankie Laine.

Order Books On-line at:
www.RichardGrudens.com
Or Fax or Call Your Order in:
Celebrity Profiles Publishing
Div. Edison & Kellogg
Box 344, Stonybrook, New York 11790
Phone: (631) 862-8555 — Fax: (631) 862-0139
Email: celebpro4@aol.com

Title	Price	Qty:
The Best Damn Trumpet Player	$15.95	
The Song Stars	$17.95	
The Music Men	$17.95	
Jukebox Saturday Night	$17.95	
Magic Moments - The Sally Bennett Story	$17.95	
Snootie Little Cutie - Connie Haines Story	$17.95	
Jerry Vale - A Singer's Life	$19.95	
The Spirit of Bob Hope - One Hundred Years - One Million Laughs	$19.95	
Bing Crosby - Crooner of the Century **Winner of the Benjamin Franklin Award 2004**	$19.95	
Chattanooga Choo Choo The Life and Times of the World Famous Glenn Miller Orchestra	$21.95	
The Italian Crooners Bedside Companion	$21.95	
Star*Dust - The Bible of the Big Bands	$39.95	
Mr. Rhythm - A Tribute to Frankie Laine	$29.95	
TOTAL - Add $5 Shipping		

Name:

Address:

City:	State:	Zip:

SHIPPING: ADD $5.00 for Priority Mail (2 days arrival time) for up to 2 books.
Enclose check or money order payable to Richard Grudens. Order will be shipped immediately

FOR CREDIT CARDS, Please fill out below form completely:

Card #

Exp. Date: Phone:

Signature:

Card Type (Please Circle): Visa — Amex — Discover — Master Card

INDEX